THE
EARNED INCOME TAX CREDIT

Antipoverty Effectiveness and Labor Market Effects

Saul D. Hoffman and Laurence S. Seidman

1990

W. E. UPJOHN INSTITUTE for Employment Research
Kalamazoo, Michigan

Library of Congress Cataloging-in-Publication Data

Hoffman, Saul D., 1949–
    The earned income tax credit : anti-poverty effectiveness and
labor market effects / Saul D. Hoffman, Laurence S. Seidman.
        p.   cm.
    Includes bibliographical references and index.
    ISBN 0-88099-096-1 (paper : acid-free)
    1. Earned income tax credit—United States. 2. Poor—United
States. 3. United States—Full employment policies.   I. Seidman,
Laurence S.   II. Title.
    HJ4653.C73H62   1990
    336.24'16'0973—dc20   90–12845
                                                                                     CIP

TP

THE INSTITUTE, a nonprofit research organization, was established on July 1, 1945.
It is an activity of the W. E. Upjohn Unemployment Trustee Corporation, which was
formed in 1932 to administer a fund set aside by the late Dr. W. E. Upjohn for the
purpose of carrying on "research into the causes and effects of unemployment and
measures for the alleviation of unemployment."

The Authors

Saul D. Hoffman is an Associate Professor of Economics at the University of Delaware where he has taught since 1977. He received his Ph.D. in Economics at the University of Michigan. His research focuses primarily on poverty and welfare policy, economic demography, and child support. His work has been published in *The American Economic Review, The Review of Economics and Statistics, The Journal of Human Resources,* and *Demography.* He is also the author of *Labor Market Economics* (Prentice-Hall, 1986).

Laurence Seidman has been at the University of Delaware since 1982. Previously, he taught at the University of Pennsylvania and Swarthmore College, and was a consultant to the Federal Reserve Bank of Philadelphia. He received his Ph.D. in economics from the University of California, Berekely, in 1974. He has published articles in *The American Economic Review, The Journal of Political Economy,* and *The Review of Economics and Statistics.* He is the author of *Saving for America's Economic Future: Parables and Policies* (M.E. Sharpe, 1990), *Macroeconomics* (Harcourt Brace Jovanovich, 1987), and *The Design of Federal Employment Programs* (D.C. Heath, 1975).

Acknowledgments

We are grateful to the W. E. Upjohn Institute for Employment Research both for their financial suppport of this project and for their many suggestions about how it might be improved. We were very fortunate to have Steve Woodbury as our project supervisor and Judy Gentry as our editor. Their efforts and talents made a genuine and much appreciated contribution to the final product.

Other scholars also provided us with important information and useful suggestions. We want to thank, especially, Gene Steuerle, Issac Shapiro, Ellen Nissenbaum, Peter Germanis, Greg Duncan, Wendell Primus, and Robert Kalish.

Finally, we benefited from the research assistance of Don Dale and the exemplary secretarial abilities of Nancy Proctor and Jane Hoback.

Contents

Tables

Figures

Policy Summary

At a time of growing consensus that conventional policy approaches to poverty via the welfare system are ineffective, the Earned Income Tax Credit (EIC) has gained increased political support and funding. Virtually all legislative programs that address the problems of poverty and welfare dependency, the authors note, now include an expanded role for EIC.

The Earned Income Tax Credit is a transfer program that operates through the income tax system to provide an income grant (technically a refundable tax credit) to low- and moderate-income working families with children. It is unique among transfer programs in that it provides its maximum credit to families with some designated positive level of earned income, but provides no benefits at all to families with no earned income. Unlike the Aid to Families with Dependent Children program, married couples are eligible for the same EIC benefits as single-parent families with the same income. In contrast to the minimum wage, the EIC is well-targetted, since it is based on a household's total annual income rather than on an individual's hourly wage. The EIC is a public policy of growing importance which is supported virtually across the political spectrum, since it is consistent with the basic principles of both a liberal and a conservative antipoverty strategy.

With the increasing concern over the well-being of the working poor in recent years, numerous proposals to expand the EIC program have been developed. In the 101st Congress, separate Senate and House bills are being considered in a House-Senate Conference Committee. The main contribution of this study is its analysis of the strengths and weaknesses of the current program and also of the likely effects of adjustments to the EIC. The authors describe the Earned Income Tax Credit as ''a policy whose time on the national agenda has clearly come.''

For Jake and Nathaniel

For Suzanna and Jesse

Introduction

The decade of the 1980s was a difficult time for policymakers concerned with the problems of poverty. The decade began with a recession that pushed the poverty rate in 1982 and 1983 to its highest level in almost 20 years. Despite the improvement in the economy since then, the poverty rate at the end of the decade was still higher than at any time during the 1970s. The 1980s also saw declining poverty rates for the elderly coincide with rising poverty rates for children. In 1987, for example, one child in five lived in poverty, and for children under age six it was almost one in four. Attention was also focused on the "underclass" (Wilson 1987), a group composed of families in concentrated poverty areas and beset with behavioral problems that allegedly left them unable to join in mainstream economic life.

Politically, the decade saw efforts to re-evaluate the success of the "welfare state" and to scale back the "safety net." There was also a growing consensus that conventional policy approaches to the poverty population via the welfare system were ineffective, or even counterproductive. Charles Murray (1984) first advanced this argument in *Losing Ground,* but it was subsequently endorsed in some respects by the Family Support Act with its emphasis on work requirements and job training.

One income transfer program that has managed not only to escape criticism but, indeed, has gained increased political support and funding is the Earned Income Tax Credit or EIC. What began as a small program in 1975 with the modest intent of offsetting Social Security payroll taxes for low-income workers with children has now become a rallying point in redirecting poverty policy. Indeed, the EIC now often seems to be the policy of choice for a wide range of problems ranging from the minimum wage ("increase the EIC instead") to child care ("adjust the EIC for family size"). Both liberals and conservatives, Democrats and Republicans, have offered legislation involving EIC adjustments and extensions.

1

What is the EIC and why is it suddenly so popular? Simply put, the EIC is an income-transfer program that operates through the tax system to provide an income grant (technically, a refundable tax credit) to low-income working households with children. In 1990, it provided a maximum of $953 and an average of over $550 to roughly 10 million families.

The popularity of the EIC program derives from its unique design that clearly distinguishes it from conventional welfare programs. Unlike the Aid to Families with Dependent Children (AFDC) program which provides maximum benefits to families who do not work, EIC provides its maximum credit to families with some designated positive level of earned income; in 1990 the maximum benefit, $953, was obtained by households with earnings between $6,810 and $10,734. Families with no earned income receive no benefits at all under EIC. Also unlike AFDC, married couples are eligible for the same benefits as single-parent families with the same income. Thus, EIC can be thought of as endorsing and financially supporting both work and marriage. The same cannot be said of AFDC.

As a way to supplement the income of low-wage workers, EIC also fares well in comparison with an increase in the minimum wage. The minimum wage is a poorly targeted program, raising wages not only for low-wage heads of household but also for many low-wage workers—primarily teenagers—in middle- and high-income families. Moreover, the minimum wage will generate involuntary unemployment whenever the legal minimum exceeds the market wage. The burden of involuntary unemployment falls heavily on low-earning households and poor teenagers.

In contrast, the EIC is well-targeted, since it is based on a household's total annual income, rather than an individual's hourly wage. Moreover, only families with children are eligible. In addition, the EIC does not generate involuntary unemployment. It may raise or lower labor supply, as we will explain in chapter 3, but at the wage that results, labor demand equals labor supply, in sharp contrast to the excess supply of labor generated by a minimum wage.

Finally, a modified EIC can be a vehicle for addressing the issue of child care. A modified EIC would adjust the benefits it provides to the size of the family and/or the age of children. Although the 1990 EIC does not adjust benefits in this way, both the Senate and the House of Representatives approved legislation in the 101st Congress that would include such a provision.

The EIC currently enjoys broad support across the political spectrum because it is consistent with the basic principles of both a "liberal" and a "conservative" antipoverty strategy. Let's consider the role of the EIC in each strategy.

The liberal envisions the EIC as a supplement to, not a replacement for, welfare. The working poor are not necessarily more worthy or deserving than the nonworking poor, but they need help and are ill-treated by AFDC, so an EIC is a useful policy. The financing of EIC should not come at the expense of welfare. Most liberals see the EIC as a complement to, not a substitute for, a relatively high minimum wage. Although some liberals recognize that a high minimum wage will reduce the number of jobs employers offer low-skilled persons, many morally object to very low wages and are impressed with the fact that the majority of low-skilled workers remain employed under a high minimum wage.

Where does the EIC fit into the larger liberal strategy? Liberals might prefer a single transfer system that targets all individuals in need regardless of work status. Also, liberals (unless they are economists) generally support a high minimum wage. But the liberal recognizes that conservative citizens who are unwilling to support welfare or a high minimum wage may be willing to support the EIC. Thus, it seems sensible to try to obtain as much conservative support as possible for the EIC, while at the same time resisting cuts in welfare and pressing for a higher minimum wage.

Conservatives, on the other hand, envision the EIC as a replacement for welfare for nonelderly, able-bodied people. They believe that the working poor are generally more worthy and deserving than the nonworking, nonelderly, able-bodied poor, and that government assistance should be targeted on them rather than those who do not work. The financing of EIC, according to conservatives, should come at the expense of welfare.

The EIC should substitute for raising the minimum wage. Permitting employers to offer jobs at low wages will result in more jobs being offered and reduce unemployment for low-skilled persons willing to work. Even if a person begins in a low-wage job, the EIC supplement will compensate for the low wage, and responsible work effort should enable the individual to earn wage increases and promotions.

Some conservatives support varying the EIC with the number of children as an alternative to child-care programs that directly subsidize providers of child care. Other conservatives oppose varying the EIC with the number of children (as well as alternative child-care programs) because they do not want to encourage poor people to have large families. To limit the total cost of EIC, most conservatives would probably support exclusion of the childless working poor.

Thus, although liberal and conservative strategies often conflict, the EIC appears to have an important role to play in each strategy.

In this monograph, we take a close and careful look at the EIC program. We look at its strengths and its weaknesses, its current effects, and also the likely effects of adjustments in the EIC program. We compare it to alternative policies intended to provide financial assistance to low income families.

As is, perhaps, inevitable in writing about important public policy issues, the policies themselves change even as one tries to analyze them. This is especially true for a policy like the Earned Income Tax Credit, whose time in the national agenda has clearly come.

When we began this research, expansion of the EIC had been considered in the 100th Congress, but no action was taken. As we worked (in 1989), the House Ways and Means Committee approved a substantial expansion of the EIC program as part of a new legislative initiative on child care. That bill, which included an increase in EIC benefits and an adjustment of benefits for family size, did not, however, reach the floor of the House during that legislative session.[1] At about the same time, the Senate passed its own child care bill, the Act for Better Child Care Services. The Senate version included a much more modest expansion of the EIC program, limited to families with children under age four. Finally, after we finished this monograph and just as this volume went to press (in the spring of 1990), the full House of Representatives approved the EIC provisions of the original Ways and Means Committee day-care bill as part of the Early Childhood Education and Development Act.

As we write this, the future of the EIC program is uncertain. There will undoubtedly be changes, but the extent of those changes is still hard to predict. The House and Senate versions differ quite signficantly in terms of EIC expansion, and a conference committee must, therefore, reconcile those differences. The House version is more than twice as expensive as the Senate version, and some compromise on the EIC expansion is a genuine possibility. And even then, a presidential veto is a distinct possibility, especially if the version reported out of conference retains many of the features of the House bill. Child-care legislation, supported by President Bush but never passed by either the House or the Senate, was similar to, but yet more modest than, the Senate version with respect to its EIC provisions.

Our approach in this monograph has been dictated, in part, by these developments. Where possible, we have tried to emphasize general principles and effects that are common to any and all EIC programs. No matter what happens to the EIC program in the Congress this session or in the future, these ideas will be valid, and, we hope, useful as well.

Where we have needed to turn to specifics—to explain, for example, *exactly* how the EIC program works—we have used the law as it stood in 1990. Where we have tried to describe who benefits from the EIC, how much in benefits different groups receive, and what effects the EIC might have on the economy, we have used the EIC law as it stood it 1988. Our reasons for doing this are explained in chapter 2. Fortunately, the EIC law in 1988 and the EIC law in 1990 are identical in all important respects. Finally, where we considered expansion and reform of the EIC program, we included among our alternatives a specification that is very similar to the legislation passed by the House of Representatives.

Chapter 1 presents an overview of the EIC: how the EIC works and what it does. Chapter 2 uses the Panel Study of Income Dynamics (PSID) data to estimate the distribution of EIC benefits in 1988 among the population and to describe some of the characteristics of the population of EIC recipients. Chapter 3 analyzes the impact of EIC on labor supply decisions. Chapter 4 compares the EIC to other antipoverty policies, including a negative income tax (NIT), welfare (AFDC), an increase in the minimum wage, and a wage-subsidy plan. Chapter 5 uses the PSID data to estimate the likely impact of a number of expansions and adjustments of the EIC program. Finally, chapter 6 considers how to increase the EIC participation rate.

NOTE

1. The bill was dropped after a split emerged among the chief sponsors over whether funding should emphasize direct grants to states or a combination of grants and tax credits (EIC) and whether church-related child care centers should be eligible for the provisions of the bill.

1
An Overview
of the
Earned Income Tax Credit

The Earned Income Tax Credit (EIC) provides assistance through the tax system to low-earning households with children. To benefit from the EIC, a household must have at least one dependent child, positive labor earnings, and total income less than a specified ceiling. Thus, the EIC helps working parents with modest incomes.

The EIC is a tax credit on the federal personal income tax. Like any tax credit, it enables an eligible household to reduce the tax it would otherwise pay. For example, if a household's tax would have been $550, but its EIC tax credit is $300, then the household must only pay $250 in tax.

Significantly, the EIC is a *refundable* tax credit. This means that if the tax credit exceeds the tax the household would otherwise owe (the tax-before-credit), then the government pays the household the difference. For example, if a household's tax-before-credit is $250, but its EIC tax credit is $550, then the government will pay the household $300.

A significant feature of the EIC is that it is based on the household, not the individual. The household's total income determines the household's EIC credit.

History of the EIC

The Earned Income Tax Credit, which emerged in the late 1980s as an important antipoverty policy, began quietly and modestly in 1975—so quietly that for many years it was virtually unnoticed by the general public, in sharp contrast to welfare (AFDC) and the minimum wage. Even many antipoverty strategists have only recently begun to emphasize the EIC.

Why was the EIC enacted? One rationale was simply to offset the Social Security payroll tax for low-income households with children. Prior to 1975, a chronic complaint against the Social Security payroll tax had been its regressivity. The payroll tax was proportional to wages up to a ceiling. Unlike the income tax, which included personal exemptions and a standard deduction, the payroll tax began with the first $100 of earnings.

But if the payroll tax was viewed as the problem, why not exempt the first few thousand dollars of wage income from payroll tax? Evidently, it was thought that this would complicate the employer's task of implementing the payroll tax for Social Security. Also, it might weaken the political claim of these workers to Social Security benefits upon retirement. So Congress decided to leave the payroll tax alone, but return the money to low-income households through a credit on the personal income tax.

Of course, some antipoverty strategists saw a more ambitious purpose for the EIC: to reward work effort and supplement the earnings of low-income households with children. Here was a policy aimed at a clientele with which many citizens sympathized: working families, including married-couple families, with modest incomes, who were often excluded from other income-transfer programs. This broader purpose yielded an important corollary: the amount of EIC supplement might exceed the amount of Social Security payroll tax. The citizenry might decide to more than compensate working parents for their payroll tax burden.

The magnitude of the EIC credit has been raised periodically since it was enacted. The maximum credit was $400 from 1976–1978, $500 from 1979–1984, $550 in 1985–1986, and has been raised each year since then. In 1990 the maximum credit was $953.

In the 101st Congress (1989-1990) both the Senate and the House of Representatives passed child-care legislation that involved a substantial expansion of the EIC program. While the specific form of the new EIC program is still uncertain (as of April 1990), it is very likely that the basic credit will be increased and will be adjusted for the number and/or age of the children in a family. The changes will probably be effective in 1991.

Mechanics of the EIC

In this section, we focus on the mechanics of how the EIC works and on its interaction with the federal income tax system. To illustrate this, we use the actual numerical parameters of the EIC program and the tax system as of 1990. Although the EIC program will probably be somewhat different in 1991 and beyond, its basic structure—the features that set EIC apart from other transfer programs—will not change. Thus, our exposition of the EIC in 1990 will apply, with only minor modifications, to the EIC program in the near future.

To simplify our exposition, we first consider a household whose income consists solely of labor earnings. In the following section, we examine how the EIC program works when a household also has nonlabor income.

There are two distinguishing features of an EIC that can be quickly grasped in figure 1.1. First, if a household has no earnings (E=0), it receives no credit (C=0), so the EIC is clearly restricted to households with labor earnings. Second, the EIC begins with a phase-in range where the credit rises as the household's labor earnings rise, and ends with a phase-out range where the credit falls as earnings continue to rise.

Figure 1.1
EIC Schedule

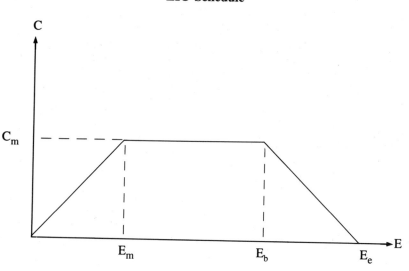

Under an EIC, the government must designate the level of earnings, E_m, at which the phase-in range ends and the credit reaches its maximum, C_m. Then, the credit must be gradually phased-out as earnings rise. The phase-out, however, need not begin immediately. As shown in figure 1.1, the EIC phase-out can be delayed by having a stationary range where the credit remains constant at C_m as the household's earnings increase. But at some earnings level E_b, the phase-out must begin, so that the credit declines with the further rise in the household's earnings until at some level of earnings E_e, the phase-out ends as the credit reaches zero.

Figure 1.2 shows the actual EIC schedule for 1990. If the household's earnings are zero, its credit is zero. When the household earns its first $100, it receives a credit of $14; it continues to receive $14 for each additional $100 of earnings until E reaches $6,810 and the credit reaches $953 (14 percent of $6,810). There is a stationary range from $6,810 to $10,734 where the credit remains $953. The phase-out begins at $10,734. The phase-out rate is 10 percent; for each additional $100 of earnings, the credit is reduced by $10. Since the maximum credit is $953, it takes $9,530 of additional earnings to completely phase-out the credit. This occurs at $E_e=\$20,264$ ($10,734+$9,530=$20,264).

Figure 1.2
EIC Schedule 1990

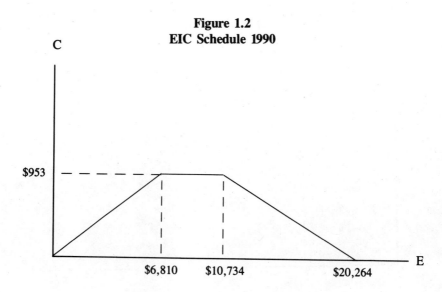

Under the 1990 EIC schedule, the credit C for a household with labor earnings E (equal to adjusted gross income AGI) is given by:[1]

$C = .14E$	if $E \leq 6{,}810$,
$C = 953$	if $6{,}810 \leq E \leq 10{,}734$,
$C = 953 - .1(E - 10{,}734)$	if $10{,}734 \leq E \leq 20{,}264$,
$C = 0$	if $E \geq 20{,}264$.

The level of earnings at which the phase-out ends, E_e, is obtained by setting $C=0$ in the third equation and solving for E:

$$0 = 953 - .1(E - 10{,}734), \text{ so } E_e = 20{,}264.$$

Under the 1986 Tax Reform Act, the phase-in and phase-out thresholds (E_m and E_b) are automatically adjusted each year for inflation.

In the phase-out range, for every additional $100 of earnings, the EIC credit is reduced $10, so the household's net gain (after earning an additional $100) is only $90. This is the same situation that an ordinary taxpayer would face if she were in a 10 percent tax bracket. Thus, it is as though the EIC recipient in the phase-out range faces a marginal tax rate (MTR) of 10 percent.

In the phase-in range, by contrast, the EIC recipient faces a negative marginal tax rate equal to –14 percent, because for every $100 of earnings, the individual gains $114. Thus, the current EIC is characterized by three marginal tax rates: –14 percent in the phase-in range, zero percent in the stationary range, and +10 percent in the phase-out range. Note that the MTR has the same magnitude as the phase-in or phase-out rate.

The EIC, however, is not the only determinant of a household's marginal tax rate. When a household's earnings reach a threshold, the household enters the positive tax system. It is the interaction of the EIC and the positive tax system that determines the household's marginal tax rate, and whether the household receives a net payment from the government (because its EIC credit exceeds its tax-before-credit), or must make a net payment to the government (because its EIC credit is less than its tax-before-credit).

The interaction of the EIC and the tax system is shown in figure 1.3 for a family of four. In 1990, with the personal exemption equal to $2,050 and the standard deduction equal to $5,450, this family enters the positive tax system when its adjusted gross income reaches $13,650 ((4 x $2,050) +$5,450=$13,650). It is then subject to a 15 percent tax rate on earnings above $13,650. When its earnings equal $16,296, its tax (before EIC credit) is $397, but its EIC credit is also $397, so $16,296 is the "break-even" earnings E_v.[2] The EIC schedule and the positive tax schedule overlap from $13,650 to $20,264.

Figure 1.3
EIC and Tax Schedules 1990

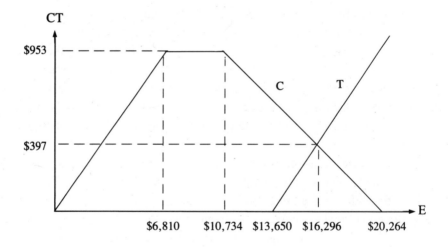

The range where the EIC phase-out overlaps with the positive tax system (E=$13,650 to E=$20,264) is especially significant. We know that the EIC phase-out alone imposes a marginal tax rate equal to the phase-out rate—10 percent—because for each additional $100 of earnings, the credit is reduced $10 so the net gain is only $90. The positive tax schedule alone imposes an MTR equal to the tax rate—15 percent—because for each additional $100 of earnings, the tax is $15 so the net gain is only $85. Together, the EIC and positive tax system impose an

MTR equal to 25 percent (10 percent+15 percent), the sum of the phase-out rate and the tax rate. For each additional $100 of earnings, the credit is reduced $10 and the tax is $15 so the net gain is only $75. Thus, in the range where the EIC and the positive tax schedule overlap, the maximum MTR occurs, and this maximum MTR equals the sum of the EIC phase-out rate and the tax rate.

As shown in figure 1.4, when earnings are between zero and $20,264, a family of four faces five different marginal tax rates due to the interaction of EIC and the positive tax system: −14 percent, 0 percent, 10 percent, 25 percent (the sum of the EIC phase-out rate of 10 percent and the tax rate of 15 percent), and 15 percent.

Figure 1.4
Marginal Tax Rates

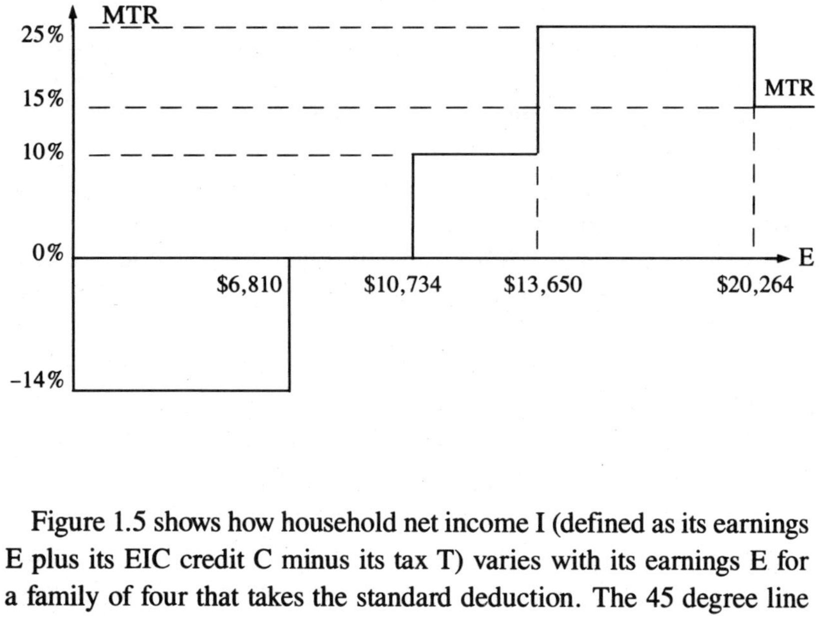

Figure 1.5 shows how household net income I (defined as its earnings E plus its EIC credit C minus its tax T) varies with its earnings E for a family of four that takes the standard deduction. The 45 degree line with a slope of 1.00 is drawn to enable a visual comparison of I and E. If the I schedule is above the 45 degree line, then I exceeds E. This is true until E reaches $16,296, the break-even earnings E_v, where the I schedule intersects the 45 degree line.

Figure 1.5
Income vs. Earnings

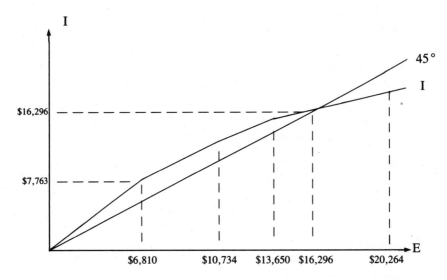

The slope of the I schedule equals (1–MTR); for example, in the range where the EIC phase-out overlaps with the positive tax schedule (E=$13,650 to E=$20,264), the slope is (1–.25)=.75, because each additional $100 of earnings results in a net gain of $75. Thus, the slope of the I schedule takes on five different values from zero to $20,264, corresponding to the five different marginal tax rates: 1.14, 1.00, .90, .75, and .85.

The EIC and Adjusted Gross Income

We now consider a complication. In fact, the EIC phase-in depends on a household's labor income, but the EIC phase-out depends on either the household's adjusted gross income or its labor income.

Adjusted gross income (AGI), as defined by the U.S. tax code, equals labor income plus capital income (property income such as interest, dividends, capital gains, or rental income) plus several items (such as unemployment compensation) minus several items (such as an individual retirement account deduction). Although a household's AGI is usually larger than its labor income, it is possible for it to be smaller due to the items that are subtracted in computing AGI.

Suppose a household has $6,810 of income in 1990. If the income is all from labor, the household obtains the maximum EIC credit, $953. If, however, the income is all from capital, the household obtains no EIC credit. Suppose instead that a household has $20,264 of income. It obtains no EIC credit, regardless of the source of the income. Thus, if the household has $6,810 of labor income, and $13,454 of capital income, it obtains no EIC credit, even though it would have obtained the maximum EIC credit, $953, if it had no capital income. Thus, an increase in capital income phases out the EIC credit just as does an increase in labor income.

The reason for the phase-in by labor earnings and phase-out by adjusted gross income or labor earnings should be evident. One purpose of the EIC is to encourage work and reward work effort. The phase-in must therefore be based on labor earnings. However, another purpose of the EIC is to assist households in financial need. The phase-out should therefore be triggered by either adjusted gross income or labor earnings.

Thus, the 1990 EIC schedule is given by:

If AGI $\leq 10,734$:

$$C = .14E \qquad \text{if } E \leq 6,810,$$
$$C = 953 \qquad \text{if } 6,810 \leq E \leq 10,734,$$
$$C = 953 - .1(E-10,734) \qquad \text{if } 10,734 \leq E \leq 20,264,$$
$$C = 0 \qquad \text{if } E \geq 20,264.$$

If AGI $\geq 10,734$:

$C = \text{Min}[C(E),C(A)]$, the smaller of $C(E)$ and $C(A)$, where $C(E)$ is the credit given by the above formula for C, and $C(A)$ is the credit given by that formula when AGI replaces E.[3]

The distinction between labor earnings and adjusted gross income justifies the overlapping of the EIC range and the positive tax range. We can explain this point by recalling our earlier example of a family of four, shown in figure 1.3.

When its earnings exceed $13,650, the family enters the positive tax system. Between E=$13,650 and E=$20,264, the family has both a tax-before-credit T and an EIC credit C. When E is less than $16,296,

C is greater than T, so the IRS makes a net payment to the family; conversely, when E is greater than $16,296, C is less than T, so the family makes a net payment to the IRS. When E equals $16,296, C equals T, so no net payment is made; we call $16,296 the break-even level of earnings.

It might be asked: Why not net out T and C in the first place? Clearly, E=$16,296 is the key level of earnings for a family of four. If E is less than $16,296, the family receives a net payment from the IRS; if E is greater than $16,296, the family makes a net payment to the IRS. We can compute the net credit for any E below $16,296, and the net tax for any E above $16,296. Why not present the household with a net EIC schedule for E less than $16,296, and a net tax schedule for E greater than $16,296? Then the household would either receive a refundable EIC credit, or pay a tax, but not both. Moreover, it would then be clear that E=$16,296 divides the population between net recipients and net payers.[4]

If the only kind of income were labor earnings, this netting out would make sense. But now consider two households. Household L earns only labor income while household K earns only capital income. Citizens may feel differently about the two kinds of income. For example, citizens may want household K to begin making a net payment to the IRS when its capital income exceeds $13,650, while they may want household L to begin making a net payment to the IRS only when its labor income exceeds $16,296. If so, then the overlapping of the EIC and tax schedules implements this preference. For household K, the C schedule in figure 1.3 is irrelevant, so it begins making a net payment to the IRS when its income exceeds $13,650.

The overlapping schedules imply that a household with only capital income begins making a net payment to the IRS at a lower income level than the household with only labor income. Citizens can specify two income levels: the income at which they want household K to begin making a net payment to the IRS ($13,650), and the income at which they want household L to begin making a net payment to the IRS ($16,296). The overlapping of the schedules then implements this preference.

Provisions of the U.S. EIC

To be eligible for the current U.S. EIC, a household must be supporting at least one child.[5] Under provisions in effect in 1990, the first child triggers the credit, but then the credit does not vary with the number of children. Under the EIC expansion considered by the 1990 Congress, beginning in 1991 the credit would vary with the number of children. In chapter 5 we will analyze the impact of varying the credit with the number of children.

On the bottom of the first page of the 1989 1040 tax return, the household is alerted: "If this line [your adjusted gross income] is less than $19,340 and a child lived with you, see 'Earned Income Credit.' " What happens if the household neglects this warning, even though it is eligible for the EIC? The IRS is instructed to check each return to determine whether the household is entitled to credit. If it is, the IRS is instructed to calculate the credit for the household, and either reduce its tax liability or pay the household the correct amount. As long as the household files a return, it should get any EIC credit to which it is entitled.

Of course, the IRS can only help a household that files a tax return. Currently, households with very low incomes are not legally required to file (for example, a gross income of $13,650 in 1990 for a married couple with two children), so there are undoubtedly households that do not receive the credit to which they are entitled. In chapter 6, we offer a proposal to address this shortcoming of the current EIC.

In theory, the household need not wait until its 1040 return is processed to receive its credit. Under the advance payment option, the credit can be received with each paycheck. In practice, however, only a small fraction of households receive credit through the advance payment option. In chapter 6, we assess the advance payment option.

The current 1040 return is virtually certain to confuse a household about how the EIC works. A clear return would first have the taxpayer calculate tax liability before credits, then let the taxpayer subtract all credits including the EIC to obtain tax owed. Tax owed would then be compared with tax withheld to determine who must write a check: the household or the government.

But, surprisingly, the EIC is not included in the credits section where it belongs. Instead, it is included later in the *payments* section, where the taxpayer is instructed to add the EIC credit to federal income tax withheld. This instruction does yield the correct answer. But it makes the EIC credit seem the same as tax withheld. In chapter 6, we suggest how the 1040 return can be revised so that a taxpayer can easily grasp the meaning of the EIC.

EIC Benefits[6]

Table 1.1 shows the evolution for selected years since 1976 of the EIC rates (phase-in rate p_i and phase-out rate p_o) and thresholds (the earnings E_m at which maximum credit C_m is reached, the earnings E_b at which the phase-out begins, and the earnings E_e at which the phase-out ends). The initial EIC was a simple symmetrical EIC with $p_i = p_o = 10$ percent, no stationary range, $E_m = E_b = \$4,000$ and $E_e = \$8,000$. Not until the Tax Reform Act of 1986 were the thresholds adjusted automatically (indexed) for inflation.

In 1979 the stationary range made its debut, and the phase-out rate p_o was made unequal to the phase-in rate p_i. But note that the phase-out rate (12.5 percent) was greater than the phase-in rate (10 percent) in 1979, while the phase-out rate since 1987 (10 percent) has been less than the phase-in rate (14 percent).

Table 1.2 shows the total amount of EIC credit and the number of families receiving credit. For 1990, it is projected that of the $5.9 billion of EIC credits, $4.8 billion will be checks written by the government to households, while $1.1 billion will reduce households' tax liability. Thus, "refundability" is extremely important. In 1990, roughly 80 percent ($4.8 billion out of $5.9 billion) of the total EIC credit would be eliminated if the EIC were not refundable.[7] Roughly 10.3 million families will receive credit, and the average credit per family will be $567.

In 1986, the number of families obtaining advance payment was very small, roughly 10,000 out of 6.3 million; the amount received was only $2.2 million out of $2.0 billion. Over 560,000 returns that did not claim credit were given credit after the IRS check of the return. Thus, about 9 percent of households who received credit (560,000 out of

Table 1.1
Earned Income Credit Parameters, Selected Years
1976–1990

Year	P_i	E_m	C_m	P_o	E_b	E_e
1976	10%	$4,000	$400	10.00%	$ 4,000	$ 8,000
1979	10	5,000	500	12.50	6,000	10,000
1985	11	5,000	550	12.22	6,500	11,000
1987	14	6,080	851	10.00	6,920	15,432
1988	14	6,240	874	10.00	9,840	18,576
1989	14	6,500	910	10.00	10,240	19,340
1990	14	6,810	953	10.00	10,730	20,264

SOURCE: Committee on Ways and Means 1990, table 15, p. 834.

Table 1.2
EIC Credit: Amounts and Coverage, Selected Years
1976–1991

Year	Total amount of credit (millions)	Number of families who received credit (thousands)	Refunded portion of credit (millions)	Average credit per family
1976	$1,295	6,473	$ 890	$200
1980	1,986	6,954	1,370	286
1984	1,638	5,759	1,162	284
1985	2,088	6,500	1,499	321
1986	2,009	6,277	1,479	320
1987	3,931	8,738	2,930	450
1988[a]	4,807	9,116	4,281	527
1989[a]	5,368	9,805	4,412	547
1990[a]	5,858	10,333	4,759	567
1991[a]	6,310	10,633	5,113	593

SOURCE: Committee on Ways and Means 1990, table 17, p. 837.
a. Projection.

6.3 million) failed to claim it on their returns. We do not have an estimate of the number of households that are entitled to credit but do not receive it because they do not file a tax return.

Table 1.3 shows how projected 1991 EIC benefits are distributed across income classes. Households with income under $20,000 receive roughly 85 percent of the total EIC credit of $6.3 billion.

Table 1.3
Projected Distribution of EIC, 1991

Income class (thousands)	All returns (thousands)	Amount of credit (millions)
$0 to $10	1,953	$1,393
$10 to $20	5,679	4,000
$20 to $30	2,768	822
$30 to $40	185	74
$40 to $50	26	12
$50 to $75	13	5
$75 to $100	6	4
$100 to $200	0	0
$200 and over	0	0
Total	10,633	6,310

SOURCE: Committee on Ways and Means 1990, table 19, p. 839.

Conclusion

The earned income tax credit (EIC) has moved from relative obscurity when it began in the mid-1970s to center stage as the 1990s begin. After more than a decade in the shadow of welfare and the minimum wage, the EIC has emerged as the antipoverty policy that commands support across the political spectrum. The key reason for this broad support is its unique design. It helps an important segment of low-income households—those who work and earn.

Chapter 1 Appendix

The Algebra of the Earned Income Tax Credit

We begin with the simpler case where adjusted gross income (AGI) equals labor earnings (E). Then we consider the case where AGI differs from E. Finally, we consider the interaction of the credit with the income tax schedule.

AGI equals E

E_m = earnings at which the phase-in range ends and the credit reaches its maximum, C_m

E_b = earnings at which the phase-out begins

E_e = earnings at which the phase-out ends as the credit reaches zero

p_i = phase-in rate

p_o = phase-out rate

The credit C for a household with labor earnings E is given by:

$C = p_i E$ if $E \le E_m$,

$C = C_m = p_i E_m$ if $E_m \le E \le E_b$,

$C = C_m - p_o(E - E_b)$ if $E_b \le E \le E_e$,

$C = 0$ if $E \ge E_e$.

To obtain E_e, set $C = C_m - p_o(E - E_b) = 0$ and solve for E to obtain:

$E_e = (C_m/p_o) + E_b = (p_i E_m/p_o) + E_b$.

AGI Differs from E

Note that although AGI is usually greater than or equal to E, it is possible for AGI to be smaller than E due to items that may be subtracted in computing AGI.

If $AGI \le E_b$:

$C = p_i E$ if $E \le E_m$,

$C = C_m = p_i E_m$ if $E_m \le E \le E_b$,

$C = C_m - p_o(E - E_b)$ if $E_b \le E \le E_e$,

$C = 0$ if $E \ge E_e$.

If $AGI \ge E_b$:

C = Min[C(E),C(A)], the smaller of C(E) and C(A), where C(E) is the credit given by the above formula for C, and C(A) is the credit given by that formula when AGI replaces E.

Interaction with the Income Tax Schedule

The tax-before-credit T is given by $T = t(E-E_x)$, where E_x is the earnings exempt from tax due to the standard deduction and personal exemptions and t is the tax rate. The break-even earnings E_v is the E at which the tax given by $T = t(E-E_x)$ equals the credit given by $C = C_m - p_o(E-E_b)$. Setting $T = C$, we solve for E to obtain

$$E_v = (tE_x + C_m + p_o E_b)/(t+p_o).$$

Income-after-tax-and-credit is $I = E - T + C$. In the range where the tax and credit interact,

$$I = E - t(E-E_x) + C_m - p_o(E-E_b), \text{ so}$$
$$I = [1-(t+p_o)]E + tE_x + C_m + p_o E_b.$$

Note that $dI/dE = [1-(t+p_o)]$.
The implicit marginal tax rate (MTR) is defined by:

$$(1-MTR) = dI/dE. \text{ Since } dI/dE = [1-(t+p_o)], \text{ MTR} = t+p_o.$$

NOTES

1. Although we have used a formula to describe the 1990 EIC schedule, the actual schedule consists of discrete brackets in a table on the 1040 personal income tax return. The formula approximates the numbers the taxpayer would actually obtain from the tax return table. The phase-out in the 1990 table actually begins at $10,730 rather than $10,734. The number that fits the formula exactly ($10,734 instead of $10,730) is presented here because it makes it easier to grasp how the EIC is constructed. An appendix to this chapter presents the algebra of the earned income tax credit.

2. We find $E_v = 16,296$ as follows. The tax T is $T = .15(E - 13,650)$. The credit C is $C = 953 - .1(E - 10,734)$. T equals C where $.15(E - 13,650) = 953 - .1(E - 10,734)$. Solving for E yields $E_v = 16,296$. A formula for E_v is given in the appendix to this chapter.

3. A general treatment is given in the appendix to this chapter.

4. The break-even level of earnings would increase with family size due to the increase in personal exemptions. But the point is still the same. It might still be asked: For each family size, why not divide the population at the break-even level of earnings for that family size, so that the household would either receive an EIC credit, or pay a tax, but not both?

5. The following are eligible for the EIC: married individuals filing a joint return who are entitled to a dependency exemption for a child; surviving spouses with a dependent child; and unmarried heads of households with a child. The household is judged to be supporting the child only if it finances more than half the expenses. If more than half of the household's income is from Aid to Families with Dependent Children (AFDC), then the household is not eligible for the EIC.

6. The material in this section draws heavily from the Committee on Ways and Means (1990).

7. The refunded portion of the credit is the portion that exceeds tax liability; it is treated as a budget outlay. The rest of the credit is classified as a tax expenditure. Thus, in recent years the budget outlay has greatly exceeded the tax expenditure for EIC.

2
A Profile
of the
EIC Population

In this chapter, we take a detailed look at the EIC recipient population in 1988. The only direct information on EIC receipt comes from published IRS tabulations on the total number of families receiving a credit, on the distribution of families across income classes, and on the average amount of credit received. But very little is known about who it is that receives EIC benefits or about how the amount of the credit varies across different groups. What fraction of working poor families receive EIC benefits? What fraction of EIC families are married couples who may receive few other benefits? What fraction of EIC families are poor? What are the average work hours and wages of workers in families receiving EIC benefits? Those are the questions we examine in this chapter.

We focus on the EIC program and the EIC population in 1988 because that was the most recent year with known EIC parameters at the time this research was conducted in mid-1989. Fortunately, the major features of the EIC program have been unchanged since 1988; the only difference is that the various income cutoff points have been adjusted annually for inflation.[1] As a result, the EIC recipient population in 1988 was probably very similar to the EIC population in 1990 and our findings for 1988 would almost certainly apply to 1990 as well.

We find that approximately one-third of all poor families and one-quarter of all black families received EIC benefits in 1988. Nevertheless, about 70 percent of the EIC population is white and three-quarters are nonpoor. The typical EIC family has a low-to-moderate income that places it above the poverty line; EIC benefits may well be the only income assistance many of these families receive. We also find that the EIC population in 1988 appeared to be working relatively long hours at relatively low wages. Finally, the average credit in 1988 was still quite low—under $500 in our data and not much above that in IRS tabulations—so the contribution of the EIC program to the economic well-being of low- and moderate-income families was certainly quite modest.

The EIC Population in 1988

Procedures

Our description of the EIC population in 1988 is based on detailed information on the income and demographic traits of a nationally representative sample of about 5,600 nonelderly households taken from the Panel Study of Income Dynamics (PSID). Because the PSID is nationally representative and provides extensive demographic and labor market information about families, it is suitable for drawing a composite picture of the EIC population.[2]

Before turning to our findings, it is important to understand the limitations of the PSID data for this purpose and how we have tried to compensate for those problems. First, the PSID does not ask directly about whether a family receives a credit through the EIC program.[3] It does, however, include information for each household on the amount of earned income, the amount of adjusted gross income, and whether or not there are children in the family—the three factors that are used to calculate the credit. Thus, it is possible to determine whether a particular family would have been eligible for EIC and to compute the amount of credit for which it would be eligible.[4]

When we do that for 1984—the most recent year for which the PSID data were available at the time of this study—and compare it to the information published by the IRS on EIC receipt in 1984, we find that the two sets of estimates are very similar. IRS tabulations show an average credit of $284 per family (the maximum credit in 1984 was $500) and a recipient population of just under 5.8 million families, while the PSID computations yield an average credit of $252 and a recipient population of about six million families. This suggests that the indirect EIC calculation that we use is quite accurate and that the PSID yields an EIC recipient population that is very close to the true EIC population.

The second problem is not as easy to resolve. Ideally, to describe the EIC population in 1988, one would use a data set that provided information for a representative national sample of families in 1988. Unfortunately, because of the time lags associated with collecting and releasing survey data, current data are not available. And since the EIC program changed substantially between 1984 and 1988, a picture of the EIC population in 1984 would tell us very little about the EIC population in 1990.

What we do, therefore, is use the 1984 PSID demographic data and "update" all 1984 income terms to 1988 values using 1984-1988 income growth factors from the Current Population Survey (CPS) to create a "pseudo-1988" PSID data set. The growth factors are disaggregated by race and by 1984 income on the basis of income quintile points reported in the 1984 and 1987 CPS. We assumed an increase in nominal income of 5 percent between 1987 and 1988.

While this is clearly an imperfect procedure, the resulting data appear reasonable.[5] For example, comparing the actual 1984 data and the pseudo-1988 data, we find that the poverty rate for nonelderly families fell about 6 percent between 1984 and 1988. That decline is comparable to the actual change over that time period.

Moreover, the two sets of EIC figures are reasonably close, especially with allowance for the fact that the reported IRS numbers are estimates. For 1988, the IRS reported an average credit per person of $527 and a recipient population of 9.1 million, while the estimate derived from the PSID for 1988 is $486 with a recipient population of about 10 million families. While we would certainly prefer to use a genuine 1988 data set, the updated 1984 data set appears to be a decent approximation. We do, however, urge reasonable caution in using the estimates. There is undoubtedly some imprecision created by our procedures.

Findings

Table 2.1 provides summary information on the fraction of families in various demographic and income categories that were eligible for the EIC in 1988. Overall, we estimate that about one family in nine (10.7 percent) received a credit. About one quarter of black families,

Table 2.1
**Proportion of Various Population Subgroups Who Received
Earned Income Credit in 1988**

All	10.7
Race	
White	8.7
Black	24.1
Poverty status	
Poor	32.0
Nonpoor	8.8
Family income	
<$10,000	27.3
$10,000–$15,000	39.1
$15,000–$20,000	13.4
$20,000–$30,000	3.7
>$30,000	1.0
Marital status	
Married	13.0
Single parent	52.0
Age of household head	
<Age 25	21.4
25–34	12.8
35–44	11.6
45–64	5.6
Number of children	
None	0
One	26.6
Two	20.2
Three or more	18.9
Residence	
Northeast	8.1
North Central	11.7
South	11.9
West	10.5
Large MSA	11.1
Small MSA	8.8
Non-MSA	12.3

SOURCE: Panel Study of Income Dynamics.

half of single-parent families, and about a third of poor families received EIC in 1988. So did nearly 9 percent of nonpoor families.

Younger families and families with one child were also more likely to receive EIC. Differences by region and MSA residence were small, with families in the Northeast least likely to receive EIC and families in non-MSAs more likely to receive EIC.

The proportion of families receiving EIC actually rises from the lowest family income bracket (<$10,000) to the second bracket ($10,000–$15,000), presumably because the first bracket includes a substantial number of families who fail to meet the earned income requirement. Among families with income above $15,000, EIC receipt falls off sharply; this reflects the income limit for EIC eligibility which in 1988 was reached at an adjusted gross income of $18,580. Note, though, that some families with substantial incomes qualify for EIC, because their adjusted gross income (on which EIC eligibility is based) is low.[6]

The most important numbers in table 2.1 are those for poor and nonpoor families. *Two-thirds of all poor, nonelderly families in 1988 were ineligible for EIC.* This should not be surprising: it is a natural consequence of the EIC requirements in conjunction with the work status and demographic status of the poverty population. We find that about a quarter of all poor, nonelderly families had children, but were ineligible for EIC because they had no earned income.[7] About another quarter had earned income but no children, and the remainder had neither earnings nor children.[8] The restriction of EIC benefits to families with children excludes over 40 percent of working poor families.

At the same time, a substantial proportion of nonpoor families received EIC in 1988. Again, there is really nothing surprising about this: it follows from the relatively low phase-out rate, the fact that credit levels are not adjusted by family size, and the occasional large differences between family income and income for tax purposes.

These nonpoor EIC recipients fall into two groups. The first group has income above the poverty line but under the 1988 EIC income maximum of $18,580. Since the poverty threshold for a family of four in 1988 was just over $12,000, it was possible to earn substantially more than the poverty line and still receive a credit. For nonpoor families in this group, 28 percent received a credit, just a bit less than for the percentage for poor families. The other nonpoor group has adjusted gross income under $18,580, but family income above that. Two percent of families with income in that range were eligible for EIC. It turns out that they account for a nontrivial portion of the EIC population.

Table 2.2 shows the average income of the EIC population in 1988. Total family income averaged just under $16,000, adjusted gross income was about $10,000, and earned income just under $9000.

Table 2.2
Mean Income of EIC Recipient Families, 1988

Total family income	$15,079
Adjusted gross income	10,034
Earned income	9,810

SOURCE: Panel Study of Income Dynamics.

Table 2.3 offers a more detailed look at the composition of the EIC population. Column (1) shows the share of EIC recipients belonging to various population subgroups, column (2) shows the average credit received by each group, and column (3) shows the share of total credits received.

The figures in column (1) reveal that EIC recipients are predominantly white (70 percent) and nonpoor (72.6 percent). Despite this latter finding, three-quarters of EIC families have incomes less than $15,000 (76 percent). At the other extreme, about one EIC family in nine has an income above $20,000, and some even have incomes above $30,000. On the whole, though, it appears that the EIC program is providing benefits primarily to moderate income, nonpoor families, precisely the group that is often excluded from most income-transfer programs.

A majority of the families have a single parent (about 80 percent of them are female-headed) and over 80 percent of the families have only

Table 2.3
EIC Receipt, Average Credit, and Share of Total Credits
by Selected Family Characteristics, 1988

	Share of EIC population (%)	Average credit ($)	Share of total credits (%)
All	100.0	486	100.0
Race			
White	70.1	478	69.2
Black	29.9	505	30.8
Poverty status			
Poor	25.4	487	25.2
Nonpoor, income <$18,580	62.6	506	64.6
Nonpoor, income >$18,580	12.0	382	10.3
Family income			
<$10,000	36.2	556	41.0
$10,000–$15,000	40.2	476	38.9
$15,000–$20,000	12.8	389	9.2
$20,000–$30,000	6.7	410	5.9
>$30,000	4.0	396	3.9
Marital status			
Married	43.5	482	43.0
Single parent	56.5	490	57.0
Age of household head			
<Age 25	18.1	528	19.7
25–34	38.0	464	36.3
35–44	26.5	520	28.3
45–64	17.4	445	15.9
Number of children			
None	0.0	0	0.0
One	48.9	495	49.8
Two	33.6	472	32.4
Three or more	17.5	487	17.2
Residence			
Northeast	16.7	508	17.4
North Central	30.6	493	31.0
South	35.1	490	35.4
West	17.7	446	16.2
Large MSA	17.9	461	17.0
Small MSA	31.5	491	31.8
Non-MSA	50.6	492	51.2

SOURCE: Panel Study of Income Dynamics.

one or two children. Geographically, the EIC population is predominantly composed of rural families (50 percent) and of families in the South
(35 percent).

There is relatively little variation in the size of the average credit
received by each group, so the share of total EIC credits received reflects
primarily each group's share of the EIC population. Thus, almost 70
percent of EIC credits go to white families, three-quarters to nonpoor
families, and over half to families in non-MSAs.

Finally, table 2.3 shows that poor families who were eligible for EIC
received, on average, a credit of $487 in 1988. Their average poverty
gap—the difference between their total income and the poverty standard for a family of their size—was almost $3,300, so that EIC
eliminated, on average, only 15 percent of the poverty gap.[9] Since EIC
benefits are positively related to earned income for much of the income
range for poor families, it follows that EIC benefits will typically be
negatively related to the poverty gap—the larger the gap, the lower the
EIC credit. It is clear that at current funding levels, EIC makes a relatively modest contribution to the economic well-being of working poor
families.

Table 2.4 examines the work hours and wage rates of EIC families.
It shows clearly that the head of an EIC household[10] is, most often,
an essentially full-time, year-round worker. Almost 60 percent worked at least 1,500 hours a year and almost a quarter reported that they
worked more than 2,080 hours—40 hours a week for 52 weeks. Wives
in EIC families worked considerably less: a bit more than one-third
did not work at all and, of those who did work, two-thirds worked less
than 1,500 hours. But family labor supply—husbands and wives
together—was substantial by any standard. The average family worked almost 1,900 hours a year, with one-third working more than 2,080
and one-eighth more than 3,000 hours.

Not surprisingly, given their considerable work hours and their low-
to-moderate incomes, the wage rates of EIC recipients were relatively
low. Approximately 40 percent of household heads and 70 percent of
working wives earned less than $5.00 an hour, while only a quarter
of the family heads and one-seventh of working wives earned as much
as $7.00 an hour. Whatever concern there may have been that the low

Table 2.4
Work Hours and Wage Rates of EIC Recipients
1988

	Share of EIC recipients (%)
Work hours – husband or single parent	
Did not work	5.1
1–500	12.5
500–1,500	25.1
1,500–2,080	34.6
>2,080	22.7
Average[a]	1,544
Work hours – wife	
Did not work	36.6
1–500	14.9
500–1,500	27.4
1,500–2,080	12.6
>2,080	8.3
Average[a]	715
Work hours – family	
1–500	11.9
500–1,500	22.7
1,500–2,080	32.4
2,080–3,000	20.6
>3,000	12.4
Average[a]	1,879
Wage rate – husband or single parent	
Did not work	5.1
<$5.00	41.0
$5.00–$7.00	29.0
>$7.00	24.9
Average	$5.89
Wage rate – wife	
Did not work	36.6
<$5.00	43.9
$5.00–$7.00	11.0
>$7.00	8.5
Average	$4.31

SOURCE: Panel Study of Income Dynamics.
a. Includes zeros.

earned incomes of EIC recipients reflected relatively low work effort rather than low wages is clearly allayed by these figures.

Summary

A number of interesting findings emerge from our profile of the 1988 EIC population. We find that the EIC program provides benefits to roughly one-third of all poor families and one-quarter of all black families. The EIC population is, however, predominantly white and non-poor. The typical EIC family has a low-to-moderate income that places it above the poverty line, and for many of these families, the EIC credit may well be the only income assistance they receive. We also find that the EIC population appears to be working relatively long hours at low wages. Finally, the average credits were quite low, so the contribution of the EIC program to the economic well-being of low- and moderate-income families is certainly quite modest.

NOTES

1. In 1988, the maximum credit was $875. The maximum earnings on which the credit could be received was $6,250 and the stationary range extended to $9,830. The credit was completely phased out at an adjusted gross income of $18,580. The phase-in and phase-out rates were 14 and 10 percent, exactly as in 1990.

2. The PSID data have been collected annually since 1968 by the University of Michigan's Institute for Social Research and have been used in countless research studies of economic well-being. Because the PSID oversamples poor families, it provides a larger-than-normal proportion of EIC-eligible families. The use of sample weights corrects for this oversampling and yields a representative national sample of the population and of EIC recipients.

3. There is no nationally representative data set that provides both specific information on EIC receipt and on characteristics of families that receive EIC.

4. We necessarily assume that every eligible family actually receives EIC. The IRS now checks all returns for EIC eligibility and computes the credit it if is not already claimed. The procedure we use will overstate receipt if some eligible families do not file tax returns.

5. It is impossible to be definitive here, since no data set containing 1988 information is currently available. CPS information for 1988 was collected in the spring of 1989 and will not be available before mid-1990.

6. The high income of some EIC-eligible families appears to reflect two general situations: (1) substantial income provided by "other family members" who may actually be filing a separate tax return; and (2) substantial nontaxable transfer income. This finding also appears in the IRS reports; see Committee on Ways and Means 1989, p. 795.

7. More accurately, there had no earned income in 1984. Since we had no information about actual employment in 1988, we assumed that individuals did not change their work status between 1984 and 1988.

8. Prior to the 1987 EIC adjustments, it was also possible for a family to be officially poor but to have an income above the maximum EIC income level and thus be income-ineligible.

9. The comparable figure from the CPS for 1986 is $4,394 for all poor families and $4,766 for poor families with children. The PSID typically finds higher reported incomes and thus lower poverty rates and poverty gaps than the CPS.

10. The PSID defines the husband as the head of a married household except in rare circumstances.

3
The Labor Supply Effects
of the EIC

In this chapter, we examine the likely effects of the EIC on the labor supply (hours of work) of EIC recipients. Labor supply effects are not only of importance in their own right—a program that reduces self-reliance is clearly a matter of concern—but also for accurately predicting program costs.[1]

That income-transfer programs might affect individual decisions about how much to work is by now well-understood. The adverse labor supply effects of the AFDC program and of the Negative Income Tax (NIT) have been widely studied and are regarded as among the more serious defects of those programs.

That EIC might also have adverse labor supply effects has not been as fully appreciated. But since EIC changes both an individual's net wage and his or her total income, it, too, provides a possible incentive for an individual to change the number of hours worked.

There are, though, some important and interesting differences between the likely labor supply effects of EIC and those of more conventional income transfer programs like AFDC and NIT. First, it is quite possible that EIC could *increase* the labor supply of workers in low-income families, something that can be said for none of the other major income-transfer programs. And second, while EIC does have some potential negative labor supply effects, they are primarily confined to workers in nonpoor families whose labor supply is already substantial. That, too, would seem to be an attractive difference between EIC and other income-transfer programs.

We estimate that in 1988 the EIC program reduced the annual hours EIC recipients worked by at most 2 or 3 percent. The small size of this effect is largely the result of the relatively modest income amounts currently offered by the program. Increases in the generosity of the program, coupled with increases in the phase-out range, would almost certainly lead to larger reductions in labor supply.

The Effect of EIC on Individual Labor Supply

We begin with a nontechnical discussion of the standard economic theory of individual labor supply in order to set the stage for evaluating the impact of EIC.[2] Readers familiar with the theory will want to skip ahead to the next section. We then turn to the details of the EIC program and look at its expected labor supply effects. Finally, we use the labor supply results from the Seattle-Denver Income Maintenance Experiments (SIME/DIME) to estimate the likely effect of the EIC program on labor supply in 1988. In chapter 5, we apply the same procedure to a set of alternative EIC plans.

The Economic Theory of Individual Labor Supply

According to the standard economic theory of individual labor supply, each individual chooses the amount of hours he or she wants to work on the basis of three general considerations: (1) the net wage rate, which is the amount by which take-home pay would increase with another hour of work; (2) the amount of nonlabor income; and (3) preferences for work vs. income. Together, these three factors lead to a "best" number of hours of work, where "best" means that the value of the income gained from an additional hour of work just offsets the value of the leisure that is given up in working that extra hour. No other choice would be preferred.

For our purposes here, the exact details of this choice are unimportant. What does matter is how this choice is likely to change when there is a change in the net wage and/or in nonlabor income. That is where EIC fits in, since, like all income-transfer programs, it does exactly that—it changes an individual's net wage and her nonlabor income.

Before turning to the specifics of EIC and the changes it causes, we need to develop the general principles. Suppose, first, that an individual's unearned income increases, but the net wage is unchanged. At the individual's current hours of work, total income (earned plus unearned) is now obviously higher than before. Both common sense and numerous research studies suggest that, in the event of a change of this kind, an individual will typically work a bit less than before.[3] More formally, economists say that the *income effect* on labor supply is negative: as unearned income goes up, the amount of hours that an individual will choose to work goes down.

The effect on desired hours of work of an increase in the net wage is more complicated because two things change simultaneously. First, the higher net wage means that an individual can now get more income per hour of leisure given up. If all other things—including income——were unchanged, it would make sense to work a bit more. Intuitively, the "price" of leisure—measured by the wage rate—is higher, and an individual would tend to "buy" less of it, which, in turn, is equivalent to working more. This effect captures the pure price effect of a wage change. It is called the *substitution effect,* and it causes a change in work hours that is in the same direction as the change in the wage rate.[4]

But other things are not equal, since the wage increase also makes an individual richer at the current hours of work. For example, a $.50 per hour wage increase for an individual working 40 hours a week makes that person exactly $20 richer, prior to any changes in labor supply. This change in income is the second effect and, exactly as in the case of an increase in unearned income, it will typically cause a decrease in work hours.

Note that in the case of an increase in the wage rate, the substitution and income effects naturally conflict. The higher wage is an incentive to work more, while the higher income is an incentive to work less. Whether an individual will work more or less when the wage increases depends on whether the substitution effect is greater than or less than the income effect.

This simple analysis is all we need to make predictions about how changes in the net wage and/or unearned income—like those caused by the EIC program—will affect an individual's labor supply choice. There are two simple "rules":

(1) An increase (decrease) in income with no change in the net wage will decrease (increase) desired labor supply. This is the income effect.

(2) An increase (decrease) in the net wage rate with no change in income (measured at the original work hours) will increase (decrease) desired labor supply. This is the substitution effect.

In order to determine the likely labor supply effects of any change, simply see which of the above conditions apply and draw the appropriate conclusion. When these changes happen in isolation, we can always make a definite prediction. When two changes happen simultaneously, the result may sometimes be indeterminate, as in the case of an increase in the wage rate that both increases the net wage and total income. But, as we will see below in the analysis of the phase-out range of the EIC, sometimes even when there are simultaneous changes, we can still be certain of the likely result.

EIC and Labor Supply

We expect EIC to affect individual labor supply choices because it alters the net wage rate an individual receives as well as his or her total income. The three ranges of the EIC—phase-in, stationary, and phase-out—have quite different labor supply effects, though, because the changes in the net wage and in nonlabor income caused by EIC are quite different in each range.

Consider, first, a low-wage worker whose household earnings before any credit place him in the EIC phase-in range (earnings less than $6,250 in 1988). With the EIC, two things happen: first, his net wage is increased by 14 percent (the EIC phase-in rate) and, second, at his current hours of work, his income is exactly 14 percent higher than before. For example, someone who was earning $4.25 an hour and working 1,250 hours a year without EIC, has, with EIC, a net wage of $4.85—$4.25 plus a $.60 per hour credit—and is $750 richer.[5]

Exactly like the case of an increase in the net wage, the effect of these changes on an individual's labor supply is uncertain. The substitution effect of the higher net wage provides an incentive to work more hours, but the income effect of more income at the current hours of work provides the opposite incentive. The incentives conflict, and on the basis of theory alone we cannot be certain which is stronger. Thus, for workers on the EIC phase-in range, EIC may increase or decrease labor supply. Although noneconomists often assume that a wage subsidy like EIC will always provide an incentive to work more, in fact, that is not necessarily so. There is no guarantee that labor supply will not decrease.

For an individual whose pre-EIC income puts her in the stationary range (income between $6,250 and $9,830 in 1988), the expected labor supply effect of EIC is unambiguous. She would receive a credit of $875 and, thus, be exactly $875 richer. But her net wage is unchanged, since another hour of work does not affect the credit she receives (unless she is earning exactly $9,830). For her, the EIC operates as a pure increase in income—it is like an increase in unearned income even though it is related to her work.[6] Thus, in this range, EIC provides an incentive to *reduce* labor supply via an income effect.

In the phase-out range (income between $9,830 and $18,580 in 1988), the labor supply prediction is also clear. Here, a worker has a lower net wage rate than in the absence of EIC, because of the 10 percent phase-out of the credit. For example, if an individual's net wage without EIC was $5.50, the net wage with EIC would be only $4.95—that is, $5.50 – .10 * $5.50—because the credit is reduced by 10 percent for each additional dollar earned. But despite this cut in the net wage, the individual is nevertheless richer because of the income received from the credit. Thus, on the phase-out range, an individual is simultaneously richer than without EIC and has a lower net wage rate. Both changes provide incentives to reduce labor supply.

This last result should not be a surprise to those familiar with the operation of means-tested income support programs—it is the standard result for a program that provides benefits to lower-income workers and then withdraws the benefits as earnings increase. The benefits make the individual richer, while the phase-out reduces the net wage. The simultaneous increase in income and cut in the net wage assures a reduction in labor supply. AFDC and NIT are the classic examples, and, indeed, the NIT experiments were conducted to provide information about how large the labor supply reductions might be.

There are several important differences, though, between the labor supply disincentives of EIC and of a traditional welfare program like AFDC. First, since the phase-out range in AFDC begins almost with the first hours of work—there is a small "earnings disregard" of $30 per month and an allowance for child care expenses—the work disincentives are concentrated on low-income workers. In contrast, in the EIC program, the phase-out range affects workers with much higher incomes and thus much higher pre-EIC work hours.

Second, the income increase and the phase-out rate in EIC are both very low, at least by the standards of other transfer programs. The current statutory phase-out rate in AFDC is 66 percent (after the $30 a month "disregard") for the first four months of work, and 100 percent thereafter. Average annual AFDC benefits per family in 1988 were $4,400 (Committee on Ways and Means 1989, table 19, p. 557) compared to less than $500 per family under EIC. Because of this, the labor supply effects of EIC will be much less serious than for more conventional income-transfer programs.

There is one final group of "workers" for whom the labor supply incentives of EIC are uniformly positive. They are easily overlooked, but they may well be important. They are workers who are not working in the absence of EIC. The most likely such group is women receiving AFDC, and for them, EIC is simply a wage increase, with no offsetting increase in income.[7] The labor supply effects for this group are unambiguously positive.

Summarizing:

(1) For a worker in a household with income that places it on the EIC phase-in range, the effects of EIC on hours of work are uncertain. Desired hours of work may increase or decrease.

(2) For a worker in a household with income that places it on the EIC stationary range, EIC reduces hours of work due to the income effect.

(3) For a worker in a household with income that places it on the EIC phase-out range, EIC reduces hours of work due to both the substitution effect and the income effect.

(4) For an individual in a household with no earned income in the absence of EIC, EIC should increase the probability of work.

Evaluating Changes in EIC

Using exactly the same labor supply analysis as above, we can predict the likely labor supply effects of *changes* in the EIC program. To assess any proposed change, simply check whether it would increase or decrease an individual's net wage and whether it would increase or decrease her income (measured at her current labor supply).

To pick a very simple example, suppose the phase-in and phase-out rates were both increased, but the income levels defining the phase-in, stationary, and phase-out ranges were kept constant. What would we expect to happen? For a worker on the phase-in range, the net wage is now higher, but so is income at the current labor supply, so labor supply could increase or decrease. On the stationary range, labor supply will definitely fall, since the credit is now larger and the net wage is unchanged. Finally, for a worker on the phase-out range, the credit is larger and the net wage lower, leading to a further reduction in labor supply.

Some effects, though, are more complex because they result in changes in the size of the population eligible for EIC. Suppose, as an example of this, that the phase-out rate was reduced but everything else remained the same. For workers on the phase-in and stationary ranges, everything is exactly as before so there would be no changes in labor supply. For workers on the phase-out range, there are conflicting effects. The lower phase-out rate increases their net wage and thus provides a labor supply incentive via the substitution effect. But, at the same time, they will receive a larger credit than before—the credit is now phased-out more slowly—and that generates an income effect that will reduce desired work. Finally, because the lower phase-out rate raises the maximum income level at which the credit is received, previously ineligible higher-income families are now eligible for EIC on the phase-out range. For these new eligibles, there is both a substitution effect, since the phase-out rate lowers the net wage, and an income effect, since they now receive a credit; both changes are incentives to reduce hours worked. Whether the total labor supply effects of this kind of change are positive or negative depends on the magnitude of the changes for the current eligibles on the phase-out range and for the new eligibles.

The Labor Supply Effects of the EIC in 1988

The theoretical predictions about the labor supply effects of EIC tell us, at most, only about its *qualitative* effects— whether labor supply is expected to increase or decrease. It does not, however, predict whether those effects are likely to be large or small. In the case of the phase-in range, where the two labor supply effects conflict, the theory does not even yield qualitative predictions. For information on the actual *quantitative* effects of EIC, we need to turn to empirical studies of individual labor supply responses to programs like EIC.

To do that, we use information on income and substitution effects estimated for low-income workers in the Seattle/Denver Income Maintenance Experiments (SIME/DIME). We then apply those estimates to the 1984 PSID data, updated to 1988 values as described in chapter 2. The SIME/DIME research provides estimates of the labor supply response of husbands, wives, and female heads per dollar of wage change (the substitution effect) and per $1000 of income change (the income effect).[8] For each working individual in a PSID family receiving an EIC credit in 1988, we first calculate the change in their net wage (relative to no EIC) and the amount of the credit they would receive, and then use those estimates to compute an expected change in labor supply.[9]

It is important to understand that we are not independently testing whether EIC causes changes in labor supply. That would be a rather formidable task that is beyond the scope of this monograph. Rather, we are assuming that the EIC recipient population reacts to the program-induced changes in the net wage and income in the same way that SIME/DIME participants reacted to the changes caused by the Negative Income Tax. Given the rather indirect link between hours of work, earned income, and receipt of the credit via the annual tax filing, it is certainly possible that workers might ignore the EIC effects altogether or perhaps regard the credit solely as an increase in income. Nevertheless, we think that treating workers as well-informed and as making purposeful decisions about labor supply is useful. It is probably prudent, though, to think of the estimates below as likely maximum responses to the current EIC program.

Our estimates are presented in table 3.1, separately for workers in each of the three EIC ranges, by wage level, and for husbands, wives, and single heads.[10] The table shows that the labor supply response is almost certainly quite small at current EIC program values. Averaging over all groups and ranges, we estimate that in 1988 the EIC program reduced labor supply of EIC recipients by just over 30 hours a year, or just over 2 percent of what labor supply would have been in the absence of an EIC program.

Table 3.1
Estimated Labor Supply Response to EIC Program, 1988

	Change in annual work hours	Percentage change	Proportion of EIC recipients
All recipients	–31.2	–2.1	100
EIC range			
Phase-in	18.4	2.2	25.2
Stationary	–35.1	–2.3	14.6
Phase-out	–51.1	–2.8	60.2
Wage rate			
< $5.00	–17.6	–1.1	48.5
$5.00 – $7.00	–36.7	–2.2	27.9
> $7.00	–52.7	–3.6	23.6
Marital status			
Husbands	–30.4	–1.6	31.5
Wives	–41.6	–3.6	21.9
Single parents	–26.9	–1.9	46.6

SOURCE: Panel Study of Income Dynamics.

Interestingly, for workers on the phase-in range, the estimated labor supply change is positive. We estimate that annual hours of work increase by 18 hours or roughly half a week's work. While this is not a large change, it is a very encouraging result—and one that was uncertain *a priori*. It may well be the first evidence of an income transfer program with any positive labor supply effects.

Because of the labor supply effect, these workers are actually earning more than they would have in the absence of the program— total earnings increase by more than the credit since labor supply increases. Since the average wage for these workers is about $4.00 per hour and their average credit is $390, the estimated labor supply increase means that the each dollar of credit received by these workers translates into a $1.18 increase in total income.[11]

For workers on the stationary and phase-out range, the estimated labor supply effects are negative, as expected. The largest negative effects are for workers on the phase-out range, because both substitution and income effects cause a decrease in hours and also because the absolute change in the wage (which determines the magnitude of the substitution effect) is usually large. Using the average wages and credit for these two groups of workers, the labor supply responses offset approximately 20 percent of the credit for workers on the stationary range and 70 percent of the credit for workers on the phase-out range.[12]

When we look at workers grouped according to their wage rates—a classification that might approximate a labor market—we find that predicted hours worked fall for all three wage groups. There is a decline even for low-wage workers, because a majority of low-wage workers are not in low-income families (i.e., phase-in level incomes). (See table 3.2 for details on the distribution of workers by wage bracket across the three EIC ranges.) The predicted decline in work hours in about 1 percent for the lowest wage group, 2 percent for workers earning between $5 and $7 per hour, and over 3.5 percent for the highest-wage group.

Table 3.2
The Distribution of Workers in EIC-Eligible Families
by Wage Rate and EIC Range, 1988

Wage level	Phase-in (%)	Stationary (%)	Phase-out (%)
< $5.00	40.2	16.8	43.1
$5.00 – $7.00	14.1	13.4	72.5
> $7.00	7.9	11.4	80.7

SOURCE: Panel Study of Income Dynamics.

Finally, the bottom portion of the table shows the predicted changes for husbands, wives, and single parents. In both absolute and percentage terms, the labor supply decline is largest for wives. This occurs both because working wives tend to be in families with income that puts them on the phase-out range and also because the SIME/DIME research found that they were most responsive to changes in the net wage and income.

What do these labor supply changes tell us? First, because EIC incorporates subsidy and taxation rates that are quite modest relative to AFDC or the NIT plans, its labor supply effects are small. The 2 percent labor supply response we found here is less than one-quarter of that found for the various NIT plans tested in the SIME/DIME research. More generous EIC plans with larger subsidy and taxation rates would be likely to have proportionately larger effects.[13]

Second, on both the phase-in and phase-out ranges, the labor supply response will *increase* the amount of credit for which a family is eligible. For workers on the phase-in range, the average 18-hour increase in labor supply would increase the credit received by about $10 (2 percent), while the labor supply response of workers on the phase-out range would increase their credit by about $30 (about 7 percent).[14]

Summary

Means-tested income-transfer programs inevitably offer incentives for individuals to reduce their work hours, and EIC is no exception. We estimate that in 1988, the EIC program reduced the annual labor supply of recipients by about 30 hours, just over 2 percent.

There are, however, two features of EIC that are unique and very attractive. Its most adverse labor supply incentives are concentrated not, as in most income-transfer programs, on workers with the weakest connection to the labor market, but on workers whose income and labor supply is substantial. Second, for workers in the poorest EIC families—those on the phase-in range—the labor supply incentives are mixed, rather than unambiguously negative. While it is not inevitable that an EIC-style wage subsidy will increase labor supply for workers on the phase-in range, our empirical estimates suggest that this is, in fact, likely to be the result.

Chapter 3 Appendix
The Labor Supply Effects of the EIC Program

Figure 3A.1 shows a standard diagram for individual labor supply analysis. Hours of work are measured along the horizontal axis and total income on the vertical axis. Since the diagram measures work hours, rather than leisure time, along the axis, the corresponding indifference curves are upward-sloping. For simplicity, we ignore the effect of taxes and other welfare programs on budget lines. We also assume that EIC does not result in any change in market wage rates.

Figure 3A.1 illustrates the effect of EIC on labor supply for a worker whose adjusted gross income in 1988 was under $6,250 and who was, therefore, on the phase-in range of the EIC. In the absence of EIC, the relevant budget line is $0B_0$; the slope of $0B_0$ is w, the market wage. Optimal labor supply is H_0, where the indifference curve and budget line are tangent.

Figure 3A.1
Labor Supply Effects of EIC
for a Worker on EIC Phase-In Range

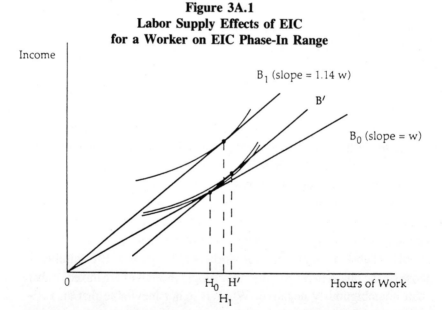

NOTE: OB_0 is budget constraint without EIC. OB_I is budget constraint with EIC.
Substitution Effect: $H_0 \rightarrow H'$; Income Effect: $H' \rightarrow H_I$; Total Effect: $H_0 \rightarrow H_I$

Figure 3A.2
Labor Supply Effects of EIC for a Worker on EIC Stationary Range

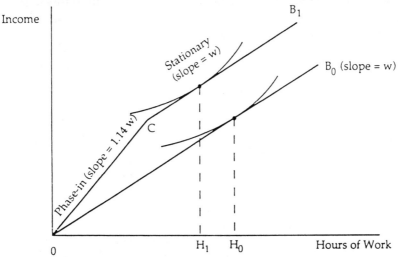

NOTE: OB_0 is budget constraint without EIC. OCB_I is budget constraint with EIC.

Income Effect = Total Effect = $H_0 \rightarrow H_I$

Figure 3A.3
Labor Supply Effects of EIC for a Worker on EIC Phase-Out Range

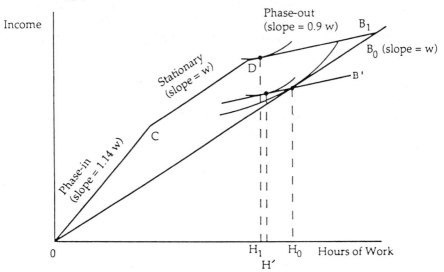

NOTE: OB_0 is budget constraint without EIC. $OCDB_I$ is budget constraint with EIC.

Substitution Effect: $H_0 \rightarrow H'$; Income Effect: $H' \rightarrow H_I$; Total Effect: $H_0 \rightarrow H_I$

In the phase-in range, EIC operates exactly like a conventional 14 percent wage increase. Thus, the EIC-inclusive budget line pivots upward to $0B_1$, whose slope is 1.14*w. Using the Slutsky decomposition, the substitution effect is measured along budget line $0B'$, which incorporates the wage subsidy (it is parallel to $0B_1$), but, for labor supply H_0, yields the original income. Faced with a higher net wage and the same total income (at H_0), an individual will typically choose to increase labor supply. In the figure, desired labor supply increases to H'. This increase from H_0 to H' reflects the substitution effect.

The income effect of the change in the net wage is measured across parallel budget lines, from $0B'$ to $0B_1$. The vertical distance between the two budget lines is precisely the amount of the credit for which the individual is eligible at current work hours (.14*wH_0 in this example). Assuming that leisure is a normal good, hours of work fall, so that the optimal hours choice along $0B_1$ will lie to the left of H' (i.e., fewer hours of work). As always, the income and substitution effects of a wage increase conflict and hours worked may rise or fall.

Whether or not the choice of desired work hours with EIC involves a decrease or increase relative to H_0 is an empirical issue. Figure 3A.1 illustrates the case where the substitution effect is greater than the income effect, so that the EIC wage subsidy increases work hours.

Figure 3A.2 provides the corresponding analysis for a worker with family income between $6,250 and $9,830. The pre-EIC budget line is again denoted as $0B_0$ and the original hours choice is H_0. With EIC, this worker faces the kinked budget line $0CB_1$. The important point is that, in the neighborhood of current labor supply, the net wage is unchanged ($0B_0$ and $0CB_1$ both have a slope of w), but total income is exactly $875 higher. The expected result is a decline in labor supply from H_0 to H_1.

Finally, the case of a worker on the EIC phase-out range is shown in figure 3A.3. The two budget lines are $0B_0$ and $0CDB_1$, and this time, in the relevant range, the EIC-inclusive budget line is both higher and flatter. The substitution effect, measured along B', causes a reduction in labor supply to H'. Here, unlike the case of a worker on the phase-in range, the income effect also causes a reduction in labor supply. Labor supply, under EIC, is shown as H_1.

NOTES

1. In the EIC program, most of the likely changes in labor supply increase the amount of credit that an individual is eligible to receive and thus increase the cost of the program.

2. A more technical analysis is given in the appendix to this chapter.

3. Intuitively, the individual "spends" some of the increase in total income on more leisure. Taking more leisure is equivalent to working fewer hours.

4. The substitution effect is measured under the hypothetical situation in which the wage changes and there is at the same time a perfectly offsetting change in nonlabor income, leaving the individual neither richer nor poorer at the current hours worked.

5. $.60 is 14 percent of $4.25. $750 equals $.60 per hour times 1,250 hours.

6. It is, however, unrelated to her hours of work at her current hours of work.

7. Technically, they are no richer at their current labor supply choice of hours.

8. We use Robins' (1985) summary of estimated income and substitution effect parameters for the SIME/DIME research. The substitution effects, measured as the expected change in annual work hours per dollar change in the wage, are –47, –85, and –75 for husbands, wives, and female heads, respectively. The corresponding income effects, per $1,000 increase in income, are –36, –47, and –50.

9. Our estimate is $\Delta H_i = b_s * \Delta W_i + b_I * \Delta I_i$, where i indexes individuals, b_s and b_I are the SIME/DIME estimated substitution and income effect parameters, respectively, ΔH is the predicted change in annual hours worked, ΔW is the change in the net wage due to EIC, and ΔI is the change in income at current labor supply and is equal to the credit received. Our approach is partial-equilibrium; we assume that the program does not change market wages. Given the current operation of the program, this is probably a reasonable assumption, but if EIC were substantially expanded, one might expect the labor supply effects to be large enough to change market wage rates.

10. For the small number of single men heading EIC families, we used the SIME/DIME labor supply response estimates for single female heads.

11. The 1.18 figure is the increase in credit plus earned income ($72) divided by the credit alone.

12. The average wages for the two groups are $5.00 and $6.00, respectively. Average credits are $874 for the stationary-range workers and $430 for those in the phase-out range.

13. See chapter 5 for further details.

14. For workers on the phase-in range, $10 is 14 percent of the additional $72 of earned income (18 hours x $4.00/hour). For workers on the phase-out range, $30 is 10 percent of the predicted $300 decrease in earnings (51 hours x $6.00/hour).

4
Comparisons with Other Antipoverty Policies

This chapter compares the Earned Income Tax Credit (EIC) with four antipoverty policies: a negative income tax, welfare (Aid to Families with Dependent Children), an increase in the minimum wage, and a wage subsidy.

Negative Income Tax

More than two decades ago, it was proposed that the tax system be used to provide cash benefits to low-income households. Instead of making a net payment to the Internal Revenue Service, a low-income household would receive a net payment from the IRS. The proposal was called a Negative Income Tax (NIT) because the household would receive cash from, rather than pay cash to, the IRS; and the amount would depend on its income. But an EIC also uses the tax system to make cash payments to low-income households. So how does an EIC differ from an NIT?

There are two crucial differences between the EIC schedule and the NIT schedule. Recall from chapter 1 the two distinguishing features of an EIC, illustrated here in figure 4.1. First, if a household has no earnings, it receives no credit, so the EIC is clearly restricted to working households. Second, the EIC begins with a phase-in range where the credit rises as the household's labor earnings rise.

As can be seen in figure 4.2, the NIT differs from the EIC in these two crucial features. If a household has no earnings, it receives the maximum credit C_m, so the NIT gives its largest credit to nonworking households. Hence, the NIT does not have a phase-in range. It may begin with a stationary range, as drawn in figure 4.2, or may simply begin with its phase-out range. Most proposed NIT plans have a small stationary range to cover work- related expenses.

Figure 4.1
EIC Schedule

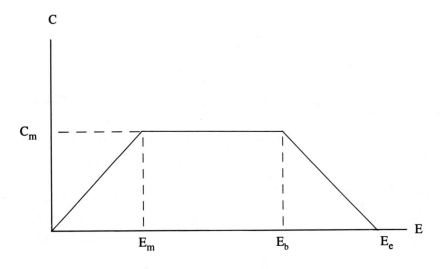

Figure 4.2
NIT Schedule

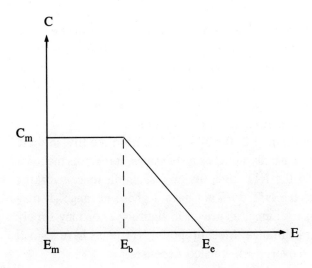

There is a simple relationship between the EIC diagram (figure 4.1) and the NIT diagram (figure 4.2). In figure 4.1, imagine moving the vertical axis to the right so it goes through point E_m (so $E_m = 0$) and then erasing everything to the left of E_m. The result would be figure 4.2, the NIT diagram. So the NIT is an EIC that omits the phase-in range.[1]

What would be the impact of an NIT on labor supply? The answer was given in chapter 3 where we analyzed the impact of an EIC on labor supply; just skip the section on the phase-in range. Just as an EIC should reduce labor supply for households in the stationary or phase-out ranges, so would an NIT.

Welfare

Both an EIC and an NIT use the tax system to assist low-income households. Welfare (Aid to Families with Dependent Children—AFDC) does not use the tax system. Yet welfare is similar to the NIT, and differs from the EIC, in the key feature of its schedule: the maximum benefit goes to the household with zero earnings, so there is no phase-in range. This feature largely reflects the historical origins of AFDC, which was included in the original Social Security Act as a way to provide assistance primarily to young widows and their children in a time when labor force participation of women with young children was not expected.

Since welfare and an NIT share this fundamental feature, how do they differ? First, an NIT would apply to all households with income below the designated standard. By contrast, AFDC largely confines assistance to single parents with children.[2] An NIT would therefore remove the incentive to become or remain a single parent in order to obtain benefits. Second, an NIT would provide cash only, and would neither impose work requirements nor offer social work services.

Whether an NIT is preferable to welfare can be debated. For our purpose, the key point is not the difference between an NIT and welfare, but the key property they share in contrast to the EIC: the NIT and welfare provide the maximum benefit to the household with zero earnings, while the EIC provides zero benefit; the NIT and welfare lack a phase-in range, a key feature of the EIC.

Minimum Wage Law

The minimum wage has two serious shortcomings in comparison with an EIC. First, raising the minimum wage reduces employment and generates involuntary unemployment. Second, many of the beneficiaries of minimum wage legislation live in relatively affluent households.

Figure 4.3 shows the impact of a minimum wage law. The legal minimum wage w* exceeds the market wage w_0 determined by supply and demand. The rise in the wage to w* reduces the total hours of labor that firms find profitable, so total hours are reduced from H_0 to H*. Workers whose hours are not reduced gain from the minimum wage law. Workers who remain employed but have hours reduced may gain or lose. Workers who are laid off or never find a job in the first place clearly lose.

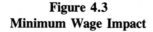

Figure 4.3
Minimum Wage Impact

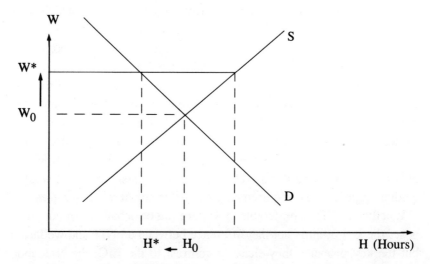

By contrast, as we explained in chapter 3, an EIC may raise or lower labor supply (depending on whether the phase-in or phase-out ranges dominate), but at the market wage that results, labor demand equals labor supply, so the EIC does not generate involuntary unemployment.

Many of the workers who benefit from raising the minimum wage are relatively affluent. One recent study (Burkhauser and Finegan 1989), using data from the Current Population Survey, estimated that if the minimum wage were raised from $3.35 to $5.05, only about 10 percent of the increased wage bill would go to low-wage workers who live in households below the poverty line, while nearly 40 percent would go to low-wage workers whose household income was at least three times the poverty line. Previous research (Gramlich 1976; Johnson and Browning 1983) also provides evidence of the weak relationship between low-wage workers and low-income families.

The minimum wage law, however, has two political advantages over the EIC. First, the EIC has a visible budgetary cost, while the minimum wage does not. Second, the EIC reduces the cost of low-skilled workers to firms, while the minimum wage raises the cost. High-wage firms that compete with low-wage firms prefer the minimum wage to EIC because it reduces competition from low-wage firms.

It should be recognized, however, that the minimum wage imposes both an invisible budgetary cost and a genuine loss on the economy. Workers who are laid off because of the minimum wage may qualify for unemployment compensation. Workers who simply do not find a job may qualify for welfare. Yet the public may not recognize that these budgetary costs are due to the minimum wage.

More important, the output of the economy is reduced by the minimum wage. Output varies directly with hours of labor. Since the minimum wage reduces total hours of work, it reduces national output. Moreover, the reduction in hours is involuntary. At the minimum wage w* in figure 4.3, workers want to supply more hours than firms demand. So the workers whose hours are reduced, or who are laid off, clearly do not prefer the enforced "leisure" to the lost income. Thus, the minimum wage imposes a genuine loss on the economy.

Wage Subsidy

A wage subsidy (WS) would pay an individual a fraction of the gap between his wage and some target wage. For example, an individual might receive a credit equal to 50 percent of the gap between his wage and $7.[3] The larger the gap (the lower the individual's wage), the larger would be the wage subsidy. If the individual's wage were $4, his credit per hour would be $1.50 (50 percent of the $3 gap); if his wage were $5, his credit per hour would be $1.00 (50 percent of the $2 gap).

A central distinction between a wage subsidy and the earned income credit is that a WS is based on the individual's wage, while the EIC is based on the household's total income. If the WS applied to all low-wage individuals, it would be subject to the same criticism as the minimum wage law: its benefits would be poorly targeted. As we just documented in our discussion of the minimum wage law, there is only a weak relationship between low-wage workers and low-income families.

This targeting problem can be significantly reduced by placing eligibility restrictions on the WS. For example, one advocate has suggested that the subsidy be limited to the principal earner in a household (the individual who earned the most money during the previous calender quarter) with dependent children.[4] This would prevent subsidy from going to nonpoor teenagers, or second earners whose primary earner has a high wage.

Nevertheless, under a wage subsidy, households with very different incomes might receive the same benefits. For example, suppose that the principal earner in households A and B each earn $5 per hour, but household A has a second earner who also earns $5 per hour, while household B does not. Household A has twice the income of household B, yet would receive the same total wage subsidy. Moreover, the wage subsidy would remain equal even if household A also had significant property income while B has none.

It would be possible, of course, to introduce further restrictions based on household income into the wage subsidy program. For example, limits on household property income might be imposed. But the result would be a hybrid subsidy, based partly on the individual's wage and partly on the household's total income, that might be difficult to understand and still be beset with unintended anomalies.

The advantage of the EIC is that it is based on household total income. Simply and automatically, the EIC takes account of multiple earners and income sources.

Besides targeting, there are two other key differences between a WS and an EIC. First, the WS credit depends exclusively on the wage rate, while the EIC credit depends on total earnings which are the product of the wage and the number of hours worked. Second, the WS phases out over its entire range; whenever the wage increases towards $7, the credit per hour is cut. By contrast, the EIC begins with a phase-in range, and may have a stationary range before its phase-out begins. What are the consequences of these two differences?

In our analysis of the EIC, we saw that a phase-out imposes a positive marginal tax rate (MTR). For example, the current EIC phase-out rate of 10 percent imposes an MTR of 10 percent because an additional $100 of earnings results in a net gain of only $90 (since the credit is cut $10). Hence, earning more—by either raising hours worked or obtaining a higher wage—is discouraged in the EIC phase-out range.

The reverse occurs in the EIC phase-in range. We saw that the phase-in imposes a "negative" MTR. For example, the current EIC phase-in rate of 14 percent imposes an MTR of -14 percent because an additional $100 of earnings results in a net gain of $114. Hence, earning more—by either raising hours worked or obtaining a higher wage—is encouraged in the EIC phase-in range.

Under a WS, the credit depends on the wage, not hours worked. So working more hours never provokes a phase-out, and is never discouraged. On the other hand, since the WS phases out over its entire range, working harder or better in order to earn a higher wage is always discouraged. In the above example, suppose a worker earns a wage increase from $4 to $5 per hour. His net gain per hour is only $.50, not $1, because his credit per hour is cut from $1.50 to $1. His income per hour (wage plus credit) rises only from $5.50 to $6. Thus, this particular wage subsidy imposes a 50 percent MTR on wage increases.

Thus, a WS never discourages more hours of work, while an EIC discourages more hours in its phase-out range. But a WS always discourages effort to earn a higher wage, while an EIC encourages such effort in its phase-in range.

Finally, there is a serious practical problem with the wage subsidy: measuring work hours accurately. Suppose an employer and employee agree on annual compensation of $10,000. Although the employee is actually required to work 2,000 hours, implying a wage of $5, the employer and employee agree to report a wage of $4 and hours of 2,500. Under the above WS example, a wage of $4 would obtain a WS credit per hour of $1.50; multiplied by 2,500 hours, the annual credit would be $3,750. If they had reported a wage of $5, the credit per hour would have been only $1; multiplied by 2,000 hours, the annual credit would have been only $2,000. Thus, by understating the wage and overstating hours worked, the employee gains $1,750 of annual credit while the employer's compensation remains $10,000.

Because it would be difficult for auditors to determine actual hours worked, especially in small firms, many employers and employees might be tempted to engage in such distortion. Monitoring wages and hours is more difficult than monitoring their product—earnings.

NOTES

1. The algebra of the NIT schedule is the same as the algebra of the EIC schedule (given in the appendix to chapter 1) with the phase-in omitted:

$$C = C_m \qquad \text{if } E \leq E_b,$$
$$C = C_m - p_o(E - E_b) \qquad \text{if } E_b \leq E \leq E_e,$$
$$C = 0 \qquad \text{if } E \geq E_e.$$

To obtain E_e, set $C = 0$ in the second equation and solve for E:

$$0 = C_m - p_o(E - E_b)$$
$$E_e = (C_m/p_o) + E_b.$$

In its phase-out range, the NIT imposes a marginal tax rate (MTR) of p_o. In the special case where the NIT phase-out begins immediately, $E_b = 0$, and $E_e = (C_m/p_o)$.

2. Married-couple families with low incomes are eligible for assistance in some states through the AFDC-UP program, but eligibility has been restrictive and participation very low. The Family Support Act of 1988 requires all states to offer the AFDC-UP program.

3. Robert Lerman, "Nonwelfare Approaches to Helping the Poor," *Focus* 11, 1 (Spring 1988).

4. Robert Lerman, "Nonwelfare Approaches to Helping the Poor," *Focus* 11, 1 (Spring 1988).

5
Revising EIC
Options and Effects

The overall picture of EIC that emerges from the previous chapters is of a program that operates quite successfully, although still on a relatively small scale. EIC is well-designed and it appears to operate efficiently. Its negative impact on individual work behavior is very small relative to other income-transfer programs. It has clear and significant advantages compared to alternative income-support programs such as minimum wage legislation, a wage-subsidy plan, and conventional welfare.

In its present form, however, EIC makes no more than a modest contribution to the well-being of low-to-moderate income families. The maximum credit received in 1988 was only $875 and the average credit actually received by an eligible family was $527.[1] (The small impact on labor supply and the small average credit received are not, of course, unrelated.) As we have emphasized several times, this average *annual* credit is not very much more than the average *monthly* income available to nonworking families in the AFDC program. Many families with a full-time worker at the minimum wage are still left far below the poverty line, even after the credit.

As part of the growing disenchantment with conventional welfare programs like AFDC and an increasing concern with the well-being of the working poor, numerous proposals to expand the EIC program have been developed in the past few years. Virtually all legislative programs to address the problems of poverty and welfare dependency now prominently include an expanded role for EIC. David Ellwood, one of the leading academic experts on the welfare system and the author of *Poor Support,* has proposed a sharp increase in the EIC subsidy rate as part of his overall welfare reform package. A proposal to adjust EIC benefits by family size was endorsed by the highly-publicized 1989 Ford Foundation Report, *The Common Good: Social Welfare and the American Future.*

61

Proposals to expand EIC often appear in the body of other legislation as the mechanism by which income-related and/or child-related transfers are made. In the 101st Congress, both the Senate and the House of Representatives considered and ultimately approved major child-care bills that featured an expansion of the EIC program. In the House of Representatives, the Early Childhood Education and Development Act would make two major changes in the program by adjusting benefits by family size and also according to the age of children.[2] The Act for Better Child Care Services, passed by the Senate, would also adjust the EIC credit rate by family size, but only for families with children under age four. For families with older children, the provisions of the EIC program would be unchanged.[3] As of this writing, the two bills were to be considered by a House-Senate Conference Committee.

In this chapter, we look at a variety of possible changes in, and expansions of, the EIC program, including variations in phase-in and phase-out rates, adjustments for family size, changes in the maximum income on which the credit is computed, and expansion of the program to poor families without children. We begin by identifying the basic trade-offs that are inherent in attempts to revise EIC. We then consider a set of specific EIC alternatives and estimate the likely impacts of these alternatives if they had been in effect in 1988. As in chapters 2 and 3, we draw our estimates from the Panel Study on Income Dynamics.

Revising EIC: Basic Issues and Problems

Most proposals for reform of EIC involve an increase in the credit rate and/or adjustments in benefit levels for family size. The logic of both changes is easy to appreciate. An across-the-board increase in EIC would help make full-time low-wage work more attractive relative to welfare. In conjunction with an increase in the minimum wage, it might also enable many low-income families to escape from poverty.[4] It is argued that family size adjustments are warranted because the maximum credit now offered is a declining fraction of the poverty standard for larger families. Relative to their needs, EIC provides less assistance to larger families.[5]

The arithmetic behind these arguments is presented in table 5.1. Column (1) shows the official 1988 poverty threshold for families ranging

Table 5.1
Low-Wage Work, EIC, and Poverty Status in 1988

Family size	Poverty threshold[a]	Year-round full-time earnings + EIC[b]	Credit as fraction of poverty threshold (%)	Post-transfer income (% of poverty threshold)
2	$ 7,701	$9,375	11.3	122
3	9,428	9,375	9.3	99
4	12,008	9,375	7.3	78
5	14,301	9,375	6.1	66

a. Estimated Poverty Thresholds, Committee on Ways and Means 1989, p. 941.
b. Assumes 2,000 hours at wage rate of $4.25.

from two to five persons; the total income for a family with a full-time low-wage worker (defined here as 2000 hours at $4.25 per hour) plus the maximum credit of $875 is given in column (2). The table shows that, as a proportion of the poverty threshold, the maximum credit falls almost in half as family size increases—from over 11 percent for a family of two to about 6 percent for a family of five. Families with two or more children remain well under the poverty threshold.[6]

The figures in the table also illustrate how just large EIC credit rates must be in order to bring larger families with low-wage workers up to the poverty threshold. Even if the credit were applied to the entire earned income of these hypothetical families (rather than just the first $6,250), the required credit rate would have to be 41 percent for a family of four and 68 percent for a family of five. These credit rates are roughly three and five times the current 14 percent rate. If, instead, the credit were calculated on only the first $6,250 of earnings, the necessary credit rates would be 56 and 93 percent, respectively.[7]

Issues in EIC Design

Expansion of EIC runs into many of the well-known conundrums that have plagued other income transfer programs, especially AFDC. While none are fatal, there are clearly trade-offs that must be recognized.

To aid in the discussion, figure 5.1 shows the 1988 EIC schedule and identifies the parameters of the schedule. C_m is the maximum credit ($875), which was received at earnings between E_m and E_b ($6,250 and $9,830 respectively in 1988). The phase-in and phase-out rates—14 and 10 percent, respectively—are reflected by the slopes of the lines. The income at which the credit is completely phased-out is E_e ($18,580 in 1988).

Consider, first, what would happen if there were an increase in the phase-in rate in order to assist low-income working families. If no other EIC parameters are changed, the higher phase-in rate means that the maximum earnings at which the credit can be received—and thus the size of the EIC-eligible population—will also rise. For example, a doubling of the EIC phase-in rate to 28 percent would extend eligibility to families with earnings up to $27,330, up from $18,580.[8] Thus, not only will poorer families now receive larger credits, but so would nonpoor families on the phase-out range, as well as yet higher-income families who were previously ineligible. As a result, a previously ineligible family with an income of $22,500 would now be eligible to receive a credit of $483. The costs of the program thus increase substantially, in large part because of the increased benefits to nonpoor and previously ineligible families.

Figure 5.1
EIC Schedule 1988

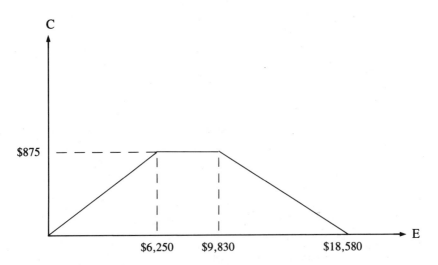

The tempting solution to this problem is to increase the phase-out range to offset the increase in the phase-in rate. In this example, a doubling of the phase-out rate to 20 percent is sufficient to maintain the maximum income for eligibility at its current level.[9] But while this solves one problem, it creates another: families on the phase-out range now face labor supply disincentives that are much more serious than before the two changes were imposed. Their net wage falls—it is now only 80 percent of the market wage[10]—but their total income (measured at their current work hours) increases because the credit they receive increases.

As was explained in chapter 3, this combination provides a dual incentive for these workers to reduce their work hours. There is also an increased work disincentive via the income effect for workers in families on the stationary range, since their credit is now larger, too. It is not even clear that workers on the phase-in range will work more as a result of the larger subsidy, since they face conflicting income and substitution effects: their net wage is higher, but so is their income.

There is no simple solution to this problem. If EIC benefits to lower-income families are to be increased, then either increased benefits will go to higher-income families and EIC expenditures will increase substantially or else moderate-income families will face increased labor supply disincentives.[11] Below we provide some quantitative information on the magnitude of the trade-offs.

EIC includes two additional program parameters that can be varied in any revision—the maximum earnings on which the credit is calculated (E_m) and the earnings at which the phase-out of the credit begins (E_b). Increasing either (or both) extends the size of the EIC-eligible population by increasing the maximum income (E_e) at which a credit can be received. An increase in E_b increases this maximum income dollar for dollar, while an increase in E_m increases it by the ratio of p_i to p_o. With the current phase-in and phase-out rates, this means that each \$1 increase in E_m increases the maximum income cutoff by \$1.40.[12]

To see clearly the effects of changes in these parameters, consider a proposal to increase E_m from its current \$6,250 to, say, \$7,500, with no change in E_b or in the phase-in or phase-out rates. This would produce a higher credit (\$175 more) for all EIC families with earnings above \$6,250 and would push the income limit for eligibility up to \$20,330.[13] Work hours for this group would probably fall slightly—they are richer at their current hours of work and their net wage is unchanged. For the poorest group of EIC workers—those with incomes below \$6,250—the increase in E_m would have no effect on either income or labor supply.

Raising E_b alone would provide no additional benefits for workers in families on the phase-in and stationary ranges. It would increase the credit only for workers in families on the phase-out range—that is, the higher-income EIC families—and would therefore provide an increased work disincentive via the income effect. It would also increase the maximum income limit for EIC eligibility.

Family Size Adjustments

Table 5.1 showed that maximum EIC benefits ranged from 11.3 percent of the poverty threshold for a family of two to 6.1 percent for a family of five. Table 5.2 shows two different ways that the maximum credit could be adjusted in order to provide benefits to all families equal to the 11.3 percent of the poverty threshold that EIC now provides for a family of two.[14] Column (3) shows how such a credit would vary with family size; it ranges from the current $875 for a family of two to $1,623 for a family of five. In column (4), we show the necessary EIC phase-in rates, assuming that the maximum income on which the credit is applied does not vary by family size. The rates start at the current 14 percent and then rise at between 3 and 5 percentage points per additional family member, reaching 26 percent for a family of five. Column (5) shows how to accomplish the same thing in a different way by varying the maximum income on which the credit can be earned rather than the credit rate. Again, there is substantial variation by family size.

Table 5.2
Alternative EIC Family Size Adjustments

Family size	Poverty threshold[a]	Maximum credit[b]	Phase-in rate[c]	Earnings threshold (E_m)
2	$ 7,701	$ 875	14.0%	$ 6,250
3	9,428	1,070	17.1	7,643
4	12,008	1,363	21.8	9,736
5	14,301	1,623	26.0	11,593

a. Estimated, 1988.
b. Maximum credit set equal to 11.3 percent of poverty threshold.
c. Assumes earnings threshold for credit equals $6,250.
d. Assumes credit rate of 14 percent.

If EIC benefits are adjusted for family size, consideration may also be given to the idea of extending eligibility to families without children. In 1988, about 40 percent of working poor households (about one-quarter of all poor households) were ineligible for EIC because they did not have children.[15] Since the poverty threshold for these smaller families is substantially less than for larger families, lower benefits would certainly be appropriate.

Revising EIC: Plans and Findings

In this section, we first describe a set of specific revisions of EIC, and then estimate the likely impact of each using the PSID data. The plans we consider are listed in table 5.3; the top half includes the EIC as it actually was in 1988 plus three variations that do not include family-size adjustments, while the bottom half includes four plans with various adjustments for family size. Because the official poverty index is based on family size, we make adjustments on that basis rather than in terms of the number of children.

Plan IA in table 5.3 is the 1988 EIC law, with a phase-in rate of 14 percent, phase-out rate of 10 percent, and a stationary range running from $6,250 to $9,830. We include it in all the analyses to provide a frame of reference. In IB, both the phase-in and phase-out rates are doubled, but the stationary range is unchanged. The maximum credit doubles, but the income limit for eligibility remains unchanged at $18,580. IC also incorporates a doubling of the phase-in rate, but the phase-out rate is kept at 10 percent. As a result, while the maximum credit for plan IC is identical to IB, the income eligibility level is substantially higher. Finally, in ID the phase-in rate is kept at the current 14 percent, but the earnings on which the credit is computed is increased by 50 percent to $9,375, and the phase-out rate is also increased by 50 percent to 15 percent. Together, these changes yield a maximum credit of $1,313 (a 50 percent increase), while keeping the size of the eligible population unchanged.

In the bottom half of the table, plan IIA applies the current EIC parameters to single parents with one child and then increases the credit rate by 4 percentage points for each additional family member through the fourth in single parent families and the fifth in married-couple families. The resulting phase-in rates—14, 18, 22, and 26 percent—are very similar to those that table 5.2 showed would, when applied to the 1988 income threshold of $6,250, produce a maximum credit that was a constant proportion of the poverty rate for families from two to five persons. This change would increase the maximum credit by $250 per person and the maximum income for EIC eligibility by $2,500 per person (up to the specified family size limits). Thus, as the table shows, a family of five or more would be eligible for EIC benefits up to an income of $26,100 in 1988.

IIB uses the same phase-in rates as in IIA, but it adjusts the phase-out rate for each family size so as to maintain the current income eligibility limit. Thus, in this version, a family of three would face a phase-in rate of 18 percent and a phase-out rate of 12.9 percent, while a family of four would have phase-in and phase-out rates of 22 and 15.7 percent, respectively.[16] IIC is identical to IIA in all respects, except that it extends eligibility to married-couple families without children, with a credit rate of 12 percent. Finally, IID keeps the credit rate at 14 percent for all families, but increases the income threshold used to compute the credit by about $1,800 per person. With these thresholds, the maximum credit by family size is exactly the same as those in IIA. Note, though, that the maximum income for eligibility is slightly higher for larger families than in IIA.[17]

Of the plans considered here, IIB is closest to the EIC expansion included in the child-care bill passed by the House of Representatives. The phase-in rates used in IIB are uniformly three points lower than in the House bill except for married couples with three children, where the rates are a point higher, and the phase-out rates considered here are slightly lower than in the House bill.[18] In both cases, however, the phase-in rate is designed so that it is 1.4 times the phase-out rate—exactly the ratio in the 1990 law—so that the resulting maximum income threshold for eligibility is the same in both plans.[19] The major difference between Plan IIB and the House version is that IIB does not include the supplemental "young child" credit, and thus is less generous.

Our estimates of the impact of all of the plans are presented in table 5.4. The procedures used are exactly the same as those used in chapter 2 to generate the descriptive information about the 1988 EIC popula-

Table 5.3
Summary of Alternative EIC Plan Characteristics

Plan	Phase-in rate (%)	Income threshold for maximum credit ($)	Maximum credit ($)	Income threshold for phase-out ($)	Phase-out rate (%)	Income threshold for eligibility ($)
No family size adjustment						
IA	14	6,250	875	9,830	10	18,580
IB	28	6,250	1,750	9,830	20	18,580
IC	28	6,250	1,750	9,830	10	27,330
ID	14	9,375	1,313	9,830	15	18,580
Family size adjustment						
IIA						
Single, 1 child	14	6,250	875	9,830	10	18,580
Single, 2 children } Married, 1 child	18	6,250	1,125	9,830	10	21,080
Single, 3+ children } Married, 2 children	22	6,250	1,375	9,830	10	23,580
Married, 3+ children	26	6,250	1,625	9,830	10	26,100
IIB						
Single, 1 child	14	6,250	8.75	9,830	10	18,580
Single, 2 children } Married, 1 child	18	6,250	1,125	9,830	12.9	18,580

Single, 3 + children } Married, 2 children }	22	6,250	1,375	9,830	15.7	18,580
Married, 3+ children	26	6,250	1,625	9,830	18.6	18,580
IIC						
Married, no child	12	6,250	750	9,830	10	17,350
Single, 1 child	14	6,250	875	9,830	10	18,580
Single, 2 children } Married, 1 child }	18	6,250	1,125	9,830	10	21,080
Single, 3+children } Married, 2 children }	22	6,250	1,375	9,830	10	23,580
Married, 3+children	26	6,250	1,625	9,830	10	26,100
IID						
Single, 1 child	14	6,250	875	9,830	10	18,580
Single, 2 children } Married, 1 child }	14	8,036	1,125	9,830	10 '	21,080
Single, 3+children } Married, 2 children }	14	9,830	1,375	10,330	10	24,070
Married, 3 + children	14	11,610	1,625	12,110	10	28,350

Table 5.4
Simulation Results for Alternative EIC Plans[a]

Plan	% families eligible	Average credit ($)	Total cost[b] ($)	Share of total credits received by		Labor supply effect	
				Poor families (%)	Families with income <$15,000 (%)	Recipients (%)	Aggregate (%)
IA	10.7	486	5.8[b]	25.4	80.8	-2.1	-.20
IB	10.7	973	11.6	25.4	80.8	-4.2	-.40
IC	17.4	919	17.8	17.0	63.4	-3.2	-.55
ID	10.7	650	7.8	22.1	81.5	-2.5	-.25
IIA	13.6	631	9.6	22.2	72.3	-2.6	-.34
IIB	10.7	640	7.6	26.9	80.6	-2.8	-.27
IIC	16.2	600	10.8	21.2	70.7	-2.5	-.39
IID	14.0	595	9.3	18.8	69.2	-2.6	-.35

a. See table 5.3 for characteristics of plans.
b. Total cost for 1988 EIC from Committee on Ways and Means, 1989, p. 793, table 12. Total cost for other plans computed relative to 1988 costs. Estimated costs do not incorporate labor supply adjustments.

tion and in chapter 3 to estimate labor supply effects. The table shows the fraction of families that would be eligible for EIC, the average credit that would be received, and the share of total EIC credits received by poor families and by families with income less than $15,000. There are also two labor supply estimates, one for recipients only and a second for the economy as a whole. The latter measure is especially useful for comparing plans in which the size of the eligible population differs. All of the findings pertain to 1988; they show what the effects of each variation would have been if they had been in effect in 1988.

The figures in the first row (IA) are for the actual 1988 EIC law. The total cost—$5.8 billion—is the IRS estimate (Committee on Ways and Means 1989, p.793); all of the other figures are from PSID tabulations.[20] Most of the numbers in the first row have been presented earlier; the last entry shows that the 1988 EIC probably reduced total labor supply in the economy by about 0.2 percent. This reflects both the coverage of the EIC in 1988 and its average effect among recipients.

Plan IB, in which the phase-in and phase-out rates are doubled, produces an average credit, total cost, and labor supply reduction that are exactly twice as high as IA, while leaving the composition of the recipient population unchanged.[21]

IC is the most expensive alternative considered. Its 28 percent phase-in rate and 10 percent phase-out rate result in an average credit of $919 and almost a doubling of the size of the EIC- eligible population, up to 17.4 percent. It is more than three times as expensive as the 1988 law and more than $6 billion more than IB.

Relative to IB, the additional costs in this plan reflect the higher credits received by families on the phase-out range and the substantial increase in the income limit for eligibility; families on the phase-in and stationary ranges receive exactly the same credit in both plans. This compositional change can be seen as well in the sharp fall in the share of total credits received by poor families and low-to-middle income families in this plan.

The possible attractiveness of a plan like IC can be seen in the next-to-last column. While its adverse effect on the labor supply of recipients is larger than in the current EIC, it is not as large as for plan IB. At the same time, though, its aggregate labor supply effect is larger than both IA and IB because the size of the recipient population is so large.[22]

This comparison illustrates the trade-off between individual and aggregate labor supply effects: changes that improve the former very often worsen the latter.

Finally, ID (raising the income level for computing the credit by 50 percent and the phase-out rate from 10 to 15 percent) is the least expensive of the plans that do not involve any family size adjustment. It provides a somewhat smaller share of credits to poor families for whom the expansion of the income level is less valuable. Because it is more generous on average than the 1988 law, it does cause a further reduction in labor supply, but the effect is quite small.

The four family-size-related plans in the bottom half of the table are, in some ways, quite similar to one another. All are more generous than the 1988 law, but there is little difference among them: average credits range from a low of $595 (IID) to a high of $640 (IIB). The predicted individual labor supply effects are also quite similar, running about 25 percent higher than in the 1988 EIC. The estimated total cost in 1988 ranges from a low of $7.8b for IIB, which has the smallest eligible population, to $10.8b for IIC, which has the largest eligible population.

Aggregate labor supply effects differ somewhat more because of differences in the size of the covered population. In this respect, IIC, which provides the broadest coverage, is the worst with an aggregate effect nearly twice as large as the 1988 law. With the exception of plan IIB, where coverage is the same as in IA, all of these plans involve aggregate labor supply effects that are substantial compared to the current law. Even so, the labor supply effects of these plans still seem relatively small. The estimated effects are less than 3 percent for recipients and less than 0.4 percent when measured on an aggregate basis.

Our estimates suggest that none of the family-size-adjusted plans involve shockingly large cost increases. We estimate that the least generous version (IIB, which increases phase-out rates along with phase-in rates) would cost about $1.8b more than the 1988 EIC law and the most generous (IIC, which does not raise phase-out rates and also includes married-couple families without children) would cost about $5b more. Comparing IIA and IIC, it appears that expansion to married-couple families without children is relatively inexpensive; we estimate a marginal cost of about $1.2b.[23]

In terms of targeting credits on poorer families, IIB is clearly the best. Indeed, it is very similar in this regard to the 1988 law, while all of the other family-size-related plans are much worse. This latter finding reflects the higher phase-in rates and low phase-out rate that are used in all of the plans except IIB.[24]

Finally, the comparison of IIA and IID—plans that offer the same maximum credit in different ways—is interesting. We find that the two plans would have very similar effects. IIA has a higher average credit, but IID has a larger eligible population, so the total costs are very close to one another. Predicted labor supply effects are identical. The one difference, which we have seen before, is that a plan like IID, that increases the income on which the credit is based, provides relatively less to poorer families than a plan like IIA, that increases credit rates.

Table 5.5 provides some additional details about the distribution of benefits under Plans IIA–IID. For each of the plans and for the 1988 EIC, the table shows the estimated average credit and the fraction of the EIC-eligible population by family size, marital status, and race.

Under the 1988 law, the pattern of credits by family size has an unexpected U-shaped pattern—the largest average benefits go to two person families and those with five or more persons. Since the 1988 law did not adjust benefits for family size in any way, this can only reflect the relationship between family income and family size.[25] The higher credits for the smallest and largest families reflect family incomes that place them relatively near the stationary range where the maximum credit is received. This shows up clearly in the PSID data: average earned income by family size is $8,557 for two person families, $10140 for three person families, $10,973 for four person families, and $9,757 for families with five or more persons.

Without exception and not surprisingly, families of three or more persons do fare better under these plans than under the 1988 law. The increases range from about 30 percentfor families of three to more than 60 percent for families for five or more. Still, the relationship between family size and family income has a major impact on the way the four family-size-adjusted plans perform. Despite the uniform family-size adjustments built into the formulas, the average credit does not, in fact, increase smoothly with family size. For three of the plans, the average

Table 5.5
Population Characteristics and Average Credit Received EIC Plans with Alternative Family Size Adjustments

Characteristic	IA		IIA		IIB		IIC		IID	
	% of EIC population	Avg. credit	% of EIC population	Avg. credit	% of EIC population	Avg. credit	% of EIC population	Avg. credit	% of EIC population	Avg. credit
All	100	486	100	631	100	640	100	600	100	595
Family size										
Two persons	27.9	504	22.1	504	27.9	504	34.7	474	21.4	504
Three persons	41.2	487	37.2	633	41.2	626	31.2	633	36.0	594
Four persons	18.9	435	24.7	622	18.9	685	20.7	622	23.8	580
Five or more	12.0	520	16.0	814	12.0	934	13.4	814	18.8	717
Marital status										
Married with children	43.5	482	52.5	670	43.5	723	44.0	670	54.1	632
Married, no children	--	--	--	--	--	--	16.2	439	--	--
Single parent, with children	56.5	489	47.5	587	56.5	577	39.8	587	45.9	551
Race										
White	70.1	478	72.9	621	70.1	637	75.4	585	73.4	590
Black	29.9	505	29.1	657	29.9	649	24.6	644	26.6	606

SOURCE: Panel Study of Income Dynamics.
NOTE: See table 5.3 for characteristics of plans.

credit actually falls as family size rises from three to four, and it then rises very sharply for families of five or more.

The different plans also yield population distributions that are quite different. IA and IIB (which are identical in terms of composition) include far fewer large families than any of the other plans. IIC, which includes childless married-couple families, is as a result much more heavily composed of small families; it is also apparent that its lower average credit is entirely due to the inclusion of these families.

The plans with higher income eligibility (IIA, IIC, and IID) have EIC populations that are more heavily composed of married-couple families, since those families typically have higher average incomes. Compared to the 1988 law, the relative proportions of married- vs. single-parent families in IIA and IID are almost exactly reversed, and IIC has an even higher proportion of married-couple families.

Finally, race differences across the plans appear to be relatively small. Average credits for black families are consistently higher than for white families, but the difference is relatively small—2 to 10 percent—and it does not vary much across the plans. Extension of eligibility to childless married-couple families appears to benefit white families much more than black families. When that change is made (plan IIC), the proportion of the EIC population that is white rises from 70 to 75 percent.

Summary

In this chapter we have explored a series of revisions and extensions of the 1988 EIC law. In its current form, EIC provides benefits that are large enough to bring a family of three persons with a full-time low-wage worker almost up to the poverty threshold, but larger families are left far below that level. Since the maximum credit takes no account of family size, EIC benefits are necessarily a much smaller fraction of the poverty threshold for larger families.

EIC can be revised along a number of dimensions. Family-size adjustments and/or across-the-board increases are especially emphasized in recent legislative proposals. While these increases may be warranted, we note that they introduce in a more serious form some of the labor supply, coverage, and cost problems that have plagued other income-transfer programs.

In the last part of the chapter, we took a close look at a serious of specific EIC alternatives. The alternatives encompassed increases in phase-in and phase-out rates, increases in coverage, and a variety of adjustments for family size. All of the plans we considered were more generous than the 1988 EIC, and all involved estimated labor supply effects that were, as a result, more negative than the 1988 law. Estimated increases in costs ranged from about $2.0b to over $12b. We estimate that adjustments for family size, along the lines of a number of recent EIC proposals, would cost about $4 billion to $5 billion more than the 1988 EIC plan.

NOTES

1. See chapter 2 for further details on the distribution of EIC benefits in 1988.

2. Effective in 1991, the EIC phase-in rate would be increased to 17 percent for a family with one child, to 21 percent for a family with two children, and to 25 percent for a family with three or more children, with associated phase-out rates of 12, 15, and 18 percent. In addition, a supplemental "young child" credit of 6 percent would be available to families with a child under the age of six; the supplemental credit would be phased-out at a rate of 4.25 percent. Thus, a family of three or more with two young children would have a combined phase-in rate of 31 percent and a combined phase-out rate of 22.25 percent. With this pattern of phase-in and phase-out rates, the maximum income for eligibility is about $21,000 in all cases; this is essentially unchanged from what the maximum would be for 1991 with the current EIC law.

3. The credit rates would be 21 percent for families with one child under age four and 24 percent for families with two or more children under age four.

4. As we have emphasized earlier, an increase in EIC is almost certainly a substitute for and preferable to an increase in the minimum wage. Recent proposals often recognize this substitutability by linking more modest increases in the minimum wage to increases in EIC.

5. The uniform treatment of families of different size presumably reflects the initial concern with offsetting payroll taxes for low-wage workers.

6. The poverty gap for this family of four is $2,634. For a family of five persons, the poverty gap is $4,927.

7. For a family of four with an earned income of $8,500, the pre-EIC poverty gap is $3,508; for a family of five, it is $5,801. The EIC credit rates in the text, applied either to $8,500 or $6,250, yield these amounts.

8. The new maximum earnings is easy to calculate. The EIC benefit formula is $C = p_i E_m - p_o (AGI - E_b)$, where AGI is adjusted gross income, p_i is the phase-in rate, p_o is the phase-out rate, and the other terms are as defined in the text. Setting the credit equal to 0 and solving for AGI (E_e in figure 5.1), we have $E_e = E_b + (p_i/p_o)E_m$. For $E_b = \$9,830$, $E_m = \$6,250$, $p_o = .10$, and $p_i = .28$, the maximum adjusted gross income at which the credit can be received is $27,330.

9. The expression for E_e in footnote 8 shows that if E_b and E_m are unchanged, E_e is unchanged as long as the ratio of p_i to p_o is constant. Thus, if both p_i and p_o are doubled (or halved, etc.), the cut-off point for eligibility will be unchanged.

10. We are continuing to ignore positive taxes. Including federal income taxes, the net wage would be only 65 percent of the market wage.

11. This problem has been debated repeatedly in the context of the design of AFDC. High benefit reduction rates limit the size of the eligible population, but generate strong labor supply disincentives for those who are eligible. Low benefit reduction rates improve labor supply incentives, but expand the pool of eligible families. Historically, the program began with high rates and low eligibility, moved to lower rates and increased eligibility, and then in the 1980s returned to something very close to the original configuration.

12. Again, this is clear from the expression for E_e in footnote 8.

13. From footnote 8, the formula for the maximum income at which the credit can be received is $E_e = E_b + (p_i/p_o)E_m$. For $E_m = \$7,500$, $E_b = \$9,830$, $p_i = .14$, and $p_o = .10$, the maximum adjusted gross income at which the credit can be received is \$20,330.

14. There is nothing magical about the 11.3 percent figure. We use it here because it is the highest percentage given to a family under the 1988 law.

15. If the thrust of EIC is to help poor working families, then there is no particularly compelling reason to exclude families without children.

16. With these changes, the ratio of phase-in to phase-out rate is the same regardless of family size. Thus, as seen earlier, the maximum income threshold will be the same for each family size.

17. This happens because the income used to compute the credit is higher than the current phase-out income threshold for the larger families. The stationary range is set equal to \$500 for these families.

18. Note that IIB bases its credits on family size rather than number of children, as in the House bill.

19. The 1.4:1 ratio holds strictly in IIB and approximately in the House bill. The two plans would have virtually identical thresholds if both were applied to 1991. The income maximums for IIB in table 5.3 refer to 1988.

20. The average credit amounts shown are from the PSID and are about 9 percent lower than those reported by the IRS.

21. The labor supply doubling reflects the linear nature of the response estimates in the SIME/DIME research.

22. These labor supply comparisons require some additional clarification. For workers on the phase-in and stationary ranges, the labor supply effects of IB and IC are identical, since the credit they receive and net wage rate are the same. For workers on the phase-out range, IC provides a larger credit and a higher net wage, both by virtue of the lower phase-out rate. This leads to conflicting income and substitution effects, so that the net effect for them is uncertain. For the newly-eligible workers in IC, predicted labor supply falls unambiguously, but the change is relatively small since the dollar amounts involved are small. The decline in the average labor supply effect per recipient is, therefore, primarily the result of extending coverage to workers with lower-than-average responses.

23. The two plans are identical except for this provision.

24. It may be inappropriate to use a fixed dollar figure (\$15,000) to evaluate a plan that is based on differences in poverty thresholds by family size. It might be better to consider the fraction of benefits received by families with an income that is less than, say, one-and-a-half times the poverty threshold.

25. If income were unrelated to family size, the average credit would not vary by family size.

6

How to Increase the EIC
Participation Rate

In this chapter, we address a central practical problem for the Earned Income Credit: How to raise the participation rate for households
entitled to EIC credit. Thanks to an IRS checking procedure, households
that file a tax return are almost certain to receive any EIC credit to which
they are entitled, even if they neglect to claim the credit. The more
serious participation problem involves households that do not file a tax
return.

Households that file a return are alerted to the EIC. At the bottom
of page 1 of both the 1989 1040 tax return and the simplified 1040A
return, it states:

> This is your adjusted gross income. If this line is less than
> $19,340 and a child lived with you, see "Earned Income
> Credit."

Page 2 of both the tax returns contains the line, "Earned income
credit." Surprisingly, this line is not in the Credits section of the return
but in the Payments section where it is added to taxes withheld, so the
taxpayer may well be confused about what the EIC is.[1] However, if
the taxpayer consults the instruction booklet, he will find how to compute his EIC using the EIC table. We suggest shifting the EIC to the
credits section of the return so that its meaning is clearer. Claiming
the EIC has not simply been left to the taxpayer. Even if a household
neglects to claim its EIC credit, it is IRS policy to check each filed tax
return for EIC eligibility and grant the credit if the household is entitled to it. Because of this important IRS policy, households that file
returns should get any EIC credit to which they are entitled, although
some may not understand why they received the credit.

The Problem of Nonfilers

But what of the household that does not file a tax return? An important achievement of the Tax Reform Act of 1986 was the exempting of many low-income households from the income tax by significantly raising the personal exemption and standard deduction. For example, in 1990 a family of four with income less than $13,650 would not owe any tax. But an ironic by-product of this attempt to help low-income households is that many may not receive the EIC credit to which they are entitled because they do not file a return. The 1040 instruction booklet encourages low-income households to file in order to obtain the EIC, but many nonfilers probably never check the 1040 instruction booklet.

In our judgment, the most important way to reach potential nonfilers is through their employers. The IRS currently tries to use employers to alert these households. The Internal Revenue Service's Circular E, the Employer's Tax Guide, is the tax instructions booklet for employers. The section entitled "Advance Payment of the Earned Income Credit" states:

> You are required to notify employees not having income tax withheld that they may be eligible for a tax refund because of the EIC. This is because the amount of EIC that exceeds tax liability is refunded. However, you will not have to notify employees claiming exemption from withholding on Form W-4.

Which employees can claim exemption from withholding on Form W-4? The Employer's Tax Guide says:

> **Exemption from income tax withholding for eligible persons.** An employee may claim to be exempt from income tax withholding because he or she had no income tax liability last year and expects none this year.

Surprisingly, then, the employer does not have to notify many employees who most need to be reached. Clearly, the employer should be required to notify these employees. The EIC section continues:

> You can notify your employees by giving them **Notice 797**, Notice of a Possible Federal Tax Refund Due to the Earned Income Credit (EIC).

Should the Advance Payment System Be Terminated?

How can employers be made more effective in distributing the EIC notice? One obstacle may be that the employer must currently accept the administrative burden of providing advance payments of the earned income tax credit. In fact, the section of the Employer's Tax Guide on the EIC begins:

> Employees eligible for the earned income credit (EIC) may either receive it on their tax returns on in advance payments during the year. Those who want it in advance must file Form W-5 with you.

The employer must then follow several single-spaced columns of instructions on how to administer advance payments. It is possible that some employers, especially in smaller business firms, will regard the advance payment system of EIC as a burden worth avoiding. The simplest way to avoid the burden is to fail to inform one's employees about the EIC, so there is no chance they will request advance payments.

How does the advance payment system work? Interested employees can file a W-5 form ("Earned Income Credit Advance Payment Certificate") with the employer. The W-5 form asks the employee whether he/she expects household adjusted gross income to be less than $20,264 (in 1990). If the employee answers "yes" to both questions, then the employee can receive advance payments of EIC.

The advance payments are a kind of negative withholding. The Employer's Tax Guide instructs the employer how to make these payments.

> **Figuring the Advance EIC Payment.** You must include the advance EIC payment with wages paid to eligible employees who have filed Form W-5. . . . Figure the amount of the payment to include in eligible employees' wage payments by using the tables . . . .
>
> Generally, employers will pay the amount of the advance EIC payment from withheld income taxes and social security taxes. . . . If for any payroll period the advance EIC payments are more than the withheld income tax and social security taxes, you may (a) reduce each advance EIC pay-

ment proportionately, or (b) elect to make full payment of the advance EIC amount and have these full amounts treated as an advance payment of the employer's tax liability.

On the W-5 form, the employee must indicate whether his/her spouse is obtaining advance EIC payments. If so, then the employer uses a table that results in a smaller advance EIC payment for that employee. The vehicle for implementing the EIC advance payment is the Employer's Quarterly Federal Tax Return.

While the current advance payment option strives for the ambitious goal of including the EIC credit with each paycheck, in practice it has hardly been utilized (only 10,000 out of 6.3 million families in 1986) so most households receive their EIC payment once a year from the IRS. Nevertheless, it is possible that an important fraction of employers may refrain from notifying their employees about the EIC in order to avoid a possible request for advance payment.

Even if the advance payments option did not deter employers from publicizing the existence of the EIC, the advance payment system runs counter to a central feature of the EIC: basing assistance on total household income. An employer can have accurate information only on the compensation he pays to one household member. He cannot know the earnings of other household members, or whether the household earns property income. Thus, it is quite possible that a household would obtain more EIC advance payment credits than its annual income would justify.

Such a low-income household would then be required to return the excess to the IRS. In practice, however, this household may find it extremely difficult to return the excess. Moreover, the household may have misunderstood the advance payment, assuming incorrectly that it need never be repaid. What penalty would the IRS levy on a household that does not return the excess?

Of course, the intent of the advance payment system is understandable: to speed payment to low-earning households that need assistance and are entitled to it under the EIC program. But this benefit must be balanced against two costs: employers may resist notifying employees about the EIC to avoid the burden of administering advance payments, and advance payment may burden some households with unexpected required repayment or punishment.

In light of these considerations, we recommend that serious consideration be given to terminating the advance payment system. Its termination will affect only a very small fraction of EIC recipients (0.2 percent in 1986). But it may significantly increase the willingness of employers to publicize the EIC to employees, thereby raising the EIC participation rate.

If the advance payment system were terminated, then the instructions to employers concerning the EIC could be greatly simplified. In place of the current detailed advance payment instructions, the Employer's Tax Guide might contain just one paragraph. In addition, this paragraph and notice 797 could be mailed out annually in the first quarter of each year. The paragraph would read:

> You are required to distribute notice 797 to each employee every January. Notice 797 informs the employee about the Earned Income Credit, a credit on the personal income tax. You have no other obligation concerning the EIC except to distribute a copy of this notice to every employee.

NOTE

1. Of course, the current method does give the correct amount still owed by the taxpayer. By inclusion in the Payments section, the EIC is treated as though it were tax already paid, just as taxes withheld are taxes already paid. By this treatment, the EIC does reduce the amount still owed by the taxpayer by the correct amount. But it would be clearer to include the EIC in the Credits section, so that it would be seen as a credit from the government to the household due to the household's labor earnings.

REFERENCES

Burkhauser, Richard and T. Aldrich Finegan. "The Minimum Wage and The Poor: The End of a Relationship." *Journal of Policy Analysis and Management* 8 (Winter 1989): 53–71.

Committee on Ways and Means, U.S. House of Representatives. *Background Material and Data on Programs within the Jurisdiction of the Committee on Ways and Means* (1990 edition).

The Common Good: Social Welfare and The American Future. New York: The Ford Foundation, 1989.

Ellwood, David T. *Poor Support.* New York: Basic Books, 1988.

Gramlich, Edward S. "Impact of Minimum Wages on Other Wages, Employment, and Family Income." *Brookings Papers on Economic Activity* (Spring 1976): 409–51.

Hendrickson, Susan E. and Isabel V. Sahill. "Assisting the Working Poor." Discussion paper. The Urban Institute, 1989.

Johnson, William R. and Edgar K. Browning. "The Distributional and Efficiency Effects of Increasing the Minimum Wage: A Simulation." *American Economic Review* 73 (March 1983): 204–11.

Murray, Charles. *Losing Ground.* New York: Basic Books, 1984.

Robins, Philip K. "A Comparison of the Labor Supply Findings from the Four Negative Income Tax Experiments." *The Journal of Human Resources* 20 (Fall 1985): 567–82.

Steuerle, C. Eugene. "Tax Credits for Workers and Children." *Journal of Economic Perspectives,* forthcoming.

_____ and Paul Willson. "The Earned Income Tax Credit." *Focus* 10,1 (Spring 1987).

Wilson, William J. *The Truly Disadvantaged.* Chicago: The University of Chicago Press, 1987.

Index

Act for Better Child Care Services (1990), S.5, 4-5, 62

Adjusted gross income (AGI): as factor in earned income of,14-16, 26; of recipients, 30; when equal to or different from earnings, 22

Aid to Families with Dependent Children (AFDC), 2; adverse effect on labor supply of, 37, 41; compared to Negative Income Tax (NIT), 55; criticism of, 61, 79n11; effect of income from, 23n5; eligibility for, 2, 60n2; phase-in/phase out range for, 41-42

Antipoverty policy: Aid to Families with Dependent Children (AFDC) as, 55; comparison of Earned Income Tax Credit program with, 53; Earned Income Tax Credit (EIC) as, 7, 8, 21

Browning, Edgar K., 57
Burkhauser, Richard, 57

Capital income, 15, 16
Child care, 2-3
Child-care legislation (proposed), 1, 2-5, 8, 17, 62; *See also* Act for Better Child Care Services (1990), S.5; Early Childhood Education and Development Act (1990), H. R.3
Children as criterion for eligibility, 17, 26, 29
Committee on Ways and Means, U. S. House of Representatives, 23n6, 35n6, 42, 73
Current Population Survey (CPS), 27

Data sources: Current Population Survey (CPS), 57; Panel Study of Income Dynamics (PSID), 26-27, 35n2, 44, 62

Early Childhood Education and Development Act (1990), H. R.3, 4-5, 8, 62, 69

Earned income: adjusted gross income factor in, 14-16, 26; basis of credit program for household, 2, 7, 26, 29, 58-59; as eligibility criterion, 29-30; estimates of effect of changes in, 64-66, 78n8; phase-in, phase-out and stationary threshholds for,9-15; wage rates for credit recipients, 32-34

Earned Income Tax Credit (EIC): adjusted gross income effect on, 14-16, 26, 30; alternative plans for, 68-77; defined, 1-3; effect on labor supply of, 37-38, 40-42, 44, 47-50, 61; eligibility for, 2, 17, 23n5, 27, 29-30, 64-65; employer role in providing information for, 82-85; estimated effect of family size adjustments, 67-68, 77; function in determining marginal tax rate, 11-14, 59; incentive and disincentive in, 15, 37, 40-42, 65-66; interpretations of, 3-4; maximum credit/benefit of, 2, 8, 35n1, 61, 62, 64, 67-68; phase-in, phase-out and stationary ranges for, 9-16, 18, 41-42, 59-60, 64; proposed expansion andreform of, 1, 2-5, 8, 17, 61-77; quantitative effects of, 44-47; recipients of credit from, 25-34; refundable tax credit of, 2, 7, 18, 21

Ellwood, David, 61

Family Support Act (1988), 1, 60n2
Finegan, T. Aldrich, 57
Ford Foundation Report, 61

Gramlich, Edward S., 57

Tax Reform Act (1986); phase-in/phase-out threshhold under, 11, 18

Unemployment, involuntary, 2

Wages. *See* Minimum wage; Wage subsidy

Wage subsidy (WS): comparison with Earned Income Tax Credit (EIC) of, 58-60; of earned income credit for low-wage workers, 2, 4, 7, 21, 25-26, 32, 34, 45, 47, 61; incentives and disincentives for, 59-60; proposed changes in eligibility for, 58-59

Welfare. *See* Aid to Families with Dependent Children (AFDC)

Wilson, William Julius, 1